WAITING
FOR THE
SUNSET

A LITTLE BIT OF THIS,
THAT, AND OTHER THINGS

TOM MCCOLLOUGH

iUniverse, Inc.
Bloomington

Waiting for the Sunset
A Little Bit of This, That, and Other Things

iUniverse books may be ordered through booksellers or by contacting:

iUniverse
1663 Liberty Drive
Bloomington, IN 47403
www.iuniverse.com
1-800-Authors (1-800-288-4677)

Because of the dynamic nature of the Internet, any Web addresses or
links contained in this book may have changed since publication and
may no longer be valid. The views expressed in this work are solely those
of the author and do not necessarily reflect the views of the publisher,
and the publisher hereby disclaims any responsibility for them.

Any people depicted in stock imagery provided by Thinkstock are models,
and such images are being used for illustrative purposes only.

Certain stock imagery © Thinkstock.

ISBN: 978-1-4759-1241-8 (sc)
ISBN: 978-1-4759-1242-5 (e)

Printed in the United States of America

iUniverse rev. date: 4/30/2012

This book is dedicated to my grandson,
Alex Fleschar.

CONTENTS

PREFACE

This is the last book I intend to publish. The general theme is biographical. The last chapter, entitled "In Sum," is several times longer than the other material and summarizes my lifetime over eighty years.

I've dedicated the book to my grandson, Alex Fleschar, because he is the recipient of some of my genes, and he is my only human link to the distant future. I worry about Alex and his generation because I am not sure that the economy will recover sufficiently to allow them the opportunities I had in the golden years of the 1950s to the 1980s. I wish him well and hope he has a long and fruitful life.

As in previous books, my daughter Janice has added several commentaries in response to mine. We have enjoyed our dialogue about the material. The psychiatrist Hugh Missildine told me that one of the hardest jobs in life is to become a friend to your adult children. Hopefully we have made it.

None of this material is very important or unique, but I do think it presents an interesting slice of life for these decades. After drafting each chapter, I attempted to edit toward simplicity, brevity, and lack of pretentiousness, but it is difficult to write a biography without using "I." Frequently I was unable to think of something amusing to add, as James Thurber surely would have.

Tom McCollough
Summer 2012

A BRIEF FAMILY LEGEND

My older twin brothers were five feet six when fully grown, stocky, and built low to the ground. They looked a little younger than they were. And they were adventuresome.

They often told the story about the first time they ever went downtown to the burlesque theater, the Trocadero (nicknamed "the Troc") when they were in high school. They went to the ticket booth and said they wanted "two children, please." The woman in the booth said, "If you are old enough to come in here, you will have to pay the adult price." They paid. End of story.

Whether this ever happened, we will never know. But knowing Jack and Jim, I suspect it did. Geez!

A DAY WITH
NOTHING TO DO

Every Monday morning, I check the calendar to see what is scheduled for the week. Meetings, doctor or dentist appointments, dinner with friends, etc. When a day is completely unscheduled, I feel a sense of relief. I have a day to sit around to do nothing if I feel like it. No pressure, no complications, and limited social interaction. This is what retirement is about.

The day proceeds. First I watch the early news on TV, followed by a quick peek at the market. Then I go to the computer to check e-mail. On a normal day, I may have twenty or more communications. At least half of the e-mail submissions are jokes, some mildly ribald and a few pornographic. I must decide which ones should go to a relative or friend and which to delete.

When I'm finished with the mail, it is time to search the Internet. A check of Abbott stock is followed by the Drudge Report to see what conservatives are pushing that day. Then the Huffington Post reveals what liberals have chosen to talk about. Recently Howard Kurtz (of Reliable Sources fame) accepted an assignment with the Daily Beast blog, so I check to see if he has a new column. After the Daily Beast, I load the *New York Times* to see whether Maureen Dowd or David Brooks have a new piece. Recently, the *Times* started charging for reading their wares, and I subscribed. I scroll down to the arts section, followed by the book section. Because I help select new books for the library, I feel obligated to stay informed about best sellers.

After scanning the *New York Times,* my choices are endless: Politico, *New York Post, Washington Post,* Instapundit, *San Francisco Chronicle,* even the Newark and Zanesville, Ohio, papers. An hour later on my day off with nothing to do, I am finished with the first round of computer searches.

By habit I print out the *USA Today* crossword puzzle. Still in my pajamas, I find a clipboard, lie down on the couch, and begin the puzzle. If it goes well, I return to the computer to print out another free daily crossword puzzle. I may start the puzzle then or put it off until later in the day. It is now time for a light breakfast.

On quiet days, I take a morning shower. That might seem effortless, but it is complicated. The glasses and watch must be removed, clean clothes laid out, a dry towel put in place, and the shower head placed so that I won't be blasted with ice-cold water. The after-shower ritual takes a while. It's a little hard to dry your back properly, so after drying everything I can reach with a towel, I lie down on my back on the bed for a few moments to let the comforter absorb water where the towel didn't reach.

Dressing should go quickly, but first I must slather the potions. Cetaphil is slathered on dry heels and legs. Underarm deodorant is a habit, but did you know that an eighty-three-year-old diabetic rarely perspires? Clothing is minimal: underwear, socks, long-sleeved t-shirt, and slacks. Shoes are donned only when it becomes necessary to leave the apartment.

At long last the day with nothing to do begins. What to do? Nap? Read? Work in the library? None of these. It's lunchtime, so the next hour and fifteen minutes is occupied by food and small talk at the dining room table. On the way back to the apartment, I pick up the mail. In our household, Marian looks at it first, weeding out catalogs and bills. Any magazines are shared with me eventually. Today there are none to fill up a do-nothing afternoon. Then the do-nothing anxiety strikes. Do something! Okay, I will read. Read what? I have no books that are unfinished. I do have H.L. Mencken's book *Prejudice* available, but that's a bit highfalutin for a day off. Instead, I decide to pull out the Kindle and finish reading last week's digital version of the *New York Review of Books* that I subscribe to. And what happens? I fall asleep for forty-five minutes. I am awakened by the sound of the cat spitting up. If Marian cleans it up, she might bend over and fall. I reach for the paper towels, but there are none. I grab some Kleenex and get to work and then find the rug cleaner and do the job right.

Suddenly the day is nearly over, and I have been busy all day on my day off. For the rest of the day, I pretend that I am doing nothing, except for a bout of solitaire, mah jong, the afternoon TV news, some straightening up around the computer desk, and that second crossword puzzle.

Here's an idea: why not write a vignette about doing nothing on my day off?

A GAGGLE OF DENTISTS
IN MY MOUTH

It's a cultural requirement. We learn at an early age that we should brush our teeth at least twice a day for at least two full minutes, without fail. So begins a lifetime ritual, providing a twinge of guilt every day of our lives. Now be honest—did you floss today? The mantra of dental hygienists everywhere is the advice that we never follow.

A dentist is chosen for us in childhood. The first visit is usually a get-acquainted visit. He or she looks in our months and hands us a sugar-free lollipop so that our fear of dentists is forever allayed. Wrong. We have a fear of dentists that lasts a lifetime. The next pediatric visit consists of cleaning, something that is supposed to happen every six months for the rest of our lives.

Cleaning visits are also something we learn to hate. The technology has improved, but not the experience. Now a hygienist starts cleaning with an ultrasonic instrument, followed by that odious scraping weapon that digs, scrapes, and probes for a half hour. Once a year it is X-ray time. Those sharp little boards are jammed into our mouths, and we breathe though our noses to suppress the gag reflex that is occurring. When the hygienist finishes the torture, the dentist arrives to examine her work and to announce that the X-ray showed some decay in teeth nineteen and thirty-two. Uh-oh, more torture ahead. Tooth decay is inevitable, and "drilling and filling" is the dentist's forte.

The practice of dentistry has changed with the advent of improved technology. Remember the crude vibration of those early drills, grinding away, generating an odor of burning bone? And the spittoons, and the little paper cups used to rinse from time to time? If you were unlucky enough to have dental problems while in the service, the drill mechanism had all the charm of a torture chamber.

Later, spittoons were replaced with high-speed drills with a water spray attached. The spittoon and paper cup were replaced with a suction device covered with gauze. The smell of ground teeth no longer annoys. Also, the profession discovered the pain-killing shot, lidocaine usually. "Do you want to be numbed?" the dentist asks. "Hell yes" is my answer. Who wants to sit there in agony? The numbing ritual includes a feeling of a swollen lip that lasts a few amusing hours.

Perhaps you can remember the names of all the dentists you have ever had. One, Joe Van Balen, found a new way to insult me. At about seventy-five years of age, I lost a tooth a few places east of my molars. He said, "At your age we don't bother building a bridge as we would with younger persons." Did he know something I didn't?

During my parents' era, dentists would favor removing all teeth and replacing them with a full plate of false teeth. Several decades ago, dentists decided that they should try to save every tooth, no matter the cost. A procedure called a root canal was born. They deadened the tooth and inserted a wire in place of the nerve. If that went bad, an oral surgeon might enter the tooth from the bottom of the root to fix the problem. Save the tooth, no matter what and at any cost.

The next advance conjured by the profession was called an implant. A regular dentist did not have the necessary skill to do the job, and the specialty of "oral and facial surgery" came into being. Those doctors have both an MD and dental certification. The implant cost becomes astronomic, approaching six thousand dollars per tooth—three thousand for the implant and another two or three thousand to put a real-looking cap on the metal stump. During the recovery phase, you must eat on the opposite side of your mouth from where the implants were embedded for three months. But think of the advantages: no decay ever, and a full set of teeth to chew on.

Now my secret: I have five implants. How long must I live to amortize that cost? Well into my nineties, I reckon. Not a bad way to ensure long life.

The process is so elaborate that after the operation the surgeon and your referring dentist send you a bouquet of flowers with a card saying, "Thank you for letting us serve you."

Hmmm. I wonder who paid for the flowers?

A SHORT POEM

The mountains are shrouded in fog today, and so am I.

Golden leaves have fallen from the trees today, and I am falling too.

A friend fell twice last week and will never return, like last winter's leaves.

But in spring, the leaves will return.

Is that a hint about immortality?

"He is in a better place now."

Does that mean heaven or eternal rest?

Neither is too bad a fate.

December 12, 2011

Note: We drove to Palo Alto to see the eye doctor. The appointment is for January 12, not December 12. I also experienced the sudden and unexpected death of "Robbie" Robinson. Hence the poem.

A STORY WITH A TWIST: PRETZELS

After dinner, Dad walked to the drugstore and came home with a hand-packed quart of Breyers ice cream. He frequently included a small pack of stick pretzels. The pretzel tray was about five inches by four, containing two dozen or so very salty thin sticks. When the ice cream was dished up, the pretzels were passed around, and we would take a handful. Instead of using a spoon, we would dig into the ice cream with the pretzel. The pleasure was a cold, sweet treat combined with a crunchy, salty taste. So began a love affair with pretzels that lingers to this day.

In Philadelphia in the forties, our pantry usually had a metal can or bag of something called beer pretzels. These were about four inches across, thick, and very hard—tooth-busters with large pieces of salt on them. Three or four was the normal dosage. A soda, lemonade, or milk accompaniment completed the snack treat.

Dad's brother, Don, bought the Anderson Pretzel Company in Lancaster, Pennsylvania. When visiting us at home, Uncle Don would bring large metal containers of them. When we visited the factory, Don let us taste a "special" pretzel that they made but did not sell. It was the size of a normal beer pretzel but less hard so they broke in shipment, and he could not market them. We loved them.

Now in old age, Marian buys me cartons of beer pretzels that I keep by my reading chair. She asks, "Have you broken a tooth yet?" "No," I answer, "but I have lost a crown or two." (Seriously!)

Companies market hard pretzels in little broken pieces flavored with mustard. I am sure that the companies invented the product to use the pieces that broke in the normal manufacturing process.

The Rold Gold division of Frito-Lay is a major producer today. The problem is that they are fake pretzels. Instead of making a pretzel by twisting a single rope of dough, they are probably extruded from a mass of unbaked dough, so they are two dimensional rather than having three dimensions. They taste okay, but we old folks who remember the real thing feel we are being cheated. Their marketing department has developed a range of variations on a theme: classics, twists, rods, tiny twists, honey mustard twists, and several others. They all taste the same, except for the flavored ones. Something is missing.

The largest company selling pretzels in 2012 is Snyder's of Hanover. Their large, hard beer pretzels look twisted from a roll of dough. Their smaller pretzels are flat and undistinguished.

When we were kids, most grocery stores sold a stick pretzel, about ten inches long and a half inch in diameter, for a penny each. One stick would pacify your pretzel desire. They were widely distributed in movie theaters and gas stations, and sold for the right price—cheap.

If you were raised on the East Coast, you may remember the soft, yeasty, bread-like pretzels sold on street corners from a push cart with the pretzels displayed in a glass case. They sold for ten cents and were offered with or without a slather of mustard. (Mustard was for hot dogs, so I ate my soft pretzels plain.) After World II, when freezers became common, they were sold frozen and partly baked. They now seem to be found only at amusement parks and state fairs. The last soft pretzels I saw in New York City were sold for over a dollar each.

Dieters proclaim that pretzels, compared to potato chips, make a calorie-light snack, whereas potato chips are rife with evil fat and outrageous calories. Or stated differently, pretzels are supposed to be guilt-free.

Now there's a twist! As the Great Gildersleeve would say, "That's a pun, son."

A TEENAGER DURING
WORLD WAR II

When the Japanese bombed Pearl Harbor, I was twelve years old. It was a Sunday afternoon when the news came, and our junior high school choir was boarding a bus to go to downtown Philadelphia to record a concert. The teachers huddled and decided to go ahead anyway, because it was unlikely that the Japanese would blow up the radio station, even though Philly had a large naval shipyard. We sang and returned home safely. My older brothers, the twins, were seventeen and a tad young to be drafted. Dad, who thought he might be called on to become a war correspondent, died about eighteen months later.

The next few days were days of confusion, patriotism, and declarations of war against Japan, Germany, and Italy. Until the war ended in 1946, my family never experienced danger of any kind, but our lives were altered. Every neighborhood was mobilized for the war effort, with civilian captains selected to monitor the blackouts and convey information to the neighbors.

We had moved into a nice fieldstone house in the suburbs. It had a recreation room in the basement that was quickly converted into a safe haven in case of attack. The room had two windows in window wells, and they were blacked out with heavy curtains so we could burn an electric light at night. Soon food and gas rationing were introduced. Our home was only several hundred yards from a bus stop, and Dad started using public transportation to go to work.

Meat was in short supply, except for a Hormel product called Spam, a very salty, ground, shaped pork product in a can two inches by four inches. Mother learned to bake it like a smoked ham, crisscrossing it with knife scars, with whole cloves inserted into the sections. Spam with sautéed apples was a weekly staple. Many night's menus consisted of a baked potato with some cheese and onion, even though cheese was rationed. Neighbors gossiped about black markets where meat could be bought without food stamps, but Mother was too conscientious to go to them.

For the next four years, our lives were dominated by war news, war activities, and war anxiety. We saved silver foil chewing gum and cigarette wrappers, bought war bonds and stamps, built small models of enemy war planes that were hung in classrooms so we would instantly identify an invader, and wrote to soldiers, known and unknown, so that every soldier would have mail at mail call.

Two of Mother's brothers were in the service. Uncle Dick Johns was eventually stationed in India, and I wrote to him every day for several years. Uncle Bob Johns was the executive officer on a mine sweeper in the navy. Mother knitted socks and scarves for the troops.

However, until the invasion of France on D-Day, the war seemed very far away. We hated and feared Hitler, Mussolini, and Hirohito, but nearly all war activities were idealized and glorious. Hollywood produced films glamorizing war and entertainment for the troops.

My twin brothers, when they came of draft age, decided to join the air force—not to fly, but to remain together in administrative roles. They were stationed in Yuma, Arizona, at an air base. When the war was over, they were still in the service and shipped to Germany. Mother and I said goodbye to them at Fort Dix, New Jersey. Mother was in tears, fearing that her boys were going into battle.

My war was the Korean War. I was drafted in 1951 and as a Medical Service Corps officer sent to Bad Nauheim, Germany. World War II ended in victory. The Korean War ended in an inglorious draw. Now we fight in Afghanistan, but the army has not contacted me to serve.

I guess gimpy eight-three-year-olds are not expected to carry backpacks and rifles.

A VERY RADICAL
RECOMMENDATION

A year or so ago I found a book entitled *1001 Books You Must Read Before You Die.* Scanning the book casually, you discover that there are many areas of great literature that you have never explored. Also, most famous and competent authors usually publish multiple books, but you have read only one of them.

When Marian and I were collecting art, we always bought more than one of every media the artist worked in: oils, pencil drawings, silk screens, etchings, etc. So it is with authors. If he or she wrote well, doesn't it follow that you should read at least two or three of their books? Willa Cather, for example. I have read *My Antonia*, *Death Comes for the Archbishop,* and *O Pioneer.* Her bibliography includes several more classic books, but I feel sated, with no need to read her exhaustively. And what about books you read fifty years ago? Might they not take on a whole new meaning if you reread them now? I read Sinclair Lewis in the 1950s. I wonder how I would react to *Main Street, Arrowsmith,* and *Babbit* today.

In the last year I have read many books that I should not have bothered with. Here is a list of three "don't waste your time" books.

A Visit from the Goon Squad

This novel describes the history of punk rock bands of the early seventies based in San Francisco. It won a Pulitzer Prize in 2010. I read the book based on several positive reviews and the fact that my daughter, Janice, was dating a punk rock guitarist in the 1970s. Don't bother.

My Lucky Life In and Out of Show Business

This maudlin, poorly written book by Dick Van Dyke has nothing to recommend it. Yes, we know that Carl Reiner was a comedic genius and that Van Dyke was a closet alcoholic. Don't bother.

The Table Comes First

This one is by the *New Yorker* writer Adam Gopnik. Here is a sentence from a glowing review: "Gopnik delves into the most burning questions of our time, including: Should a Manhattanite bother to find a chicken killed in the Bronx?" The answer is no. Don't bother.

The lesson to be learned is that we should never buy a book on impulse, no matter how fabulously a *New York Times* reviewer has gushed. You don't have any time to waste. Read only books that might enrich your life.

By now you may have wondered what my radical recommendation is. Simple: pass a law forbidding the publication of any further books printed on paper. We have enough books on paper to last us the rest of our lives. Let's assume it takes four days to read most books. Reading 1,001 books would take me an additional eleven years. Assuming I live until I am ninety-three, this estimate does not include rereading any books I love.

"Oh," you say, "no one will agree to stop publishing books." Why not? Think of the trees you will save. According to the Canadian Environmental Agency, "On average a mature tree produces nearly ten pounds of oxygen a year." Two trees can support a family of four.

In 2009, America published 288,355 new books or editions. Whoa. Just stop. Besides, have you noticed the enormous growth of e-books? We have all the books in print you and I will ever need. Let authors write all they want, but put their output on the Internet, for heaven's sake.

In the last month I have read *Thinking, Fast and Slow* by a Nobel Prize winner and *Swerve* about the rediscovery of a prophetic ancient poem by Lucretius. Don't bother.

Damn those gushing *New York Times* reviewers!

LEARNING TO LOVE BOOKS

By Janice Hudson

I will never forget a moment between my husband Mark and myself. It was early in our relationship. One afternoon, I was reading a book. He looked confused and asked, "What are you doing?"

"Reading a book," I replied.

"Why are you doing that?" he asked.

"Uh, for fun?" I answered.

He was never encouraged to read as a child. His family didn't read for recreation. To him, reading was a chore that was delegated by school. He had never read for fun. He now loves to read.

Our family always had books—lots of them. Mom always read to us at bedtime, one chapter at a time. My sister and I would howl for her to read another chapter, which meant we could stay up later, but we also wanted to find out what happened next. Winnie the Pooh and Grimm's fairy tales were on the bedtime reading list. Somehow the book of Mother Goose rhymes, one of our favorites, has survived a zillion moves and now resides on my bookshelf.

It is tattered and worn from our little fingers turning its pages over and over.

Both my parents were readers, and the house was filled with all sorts of books. They subscribed to the Time–Life nature series, and Liz and I pored over them for hours. Dad loved art, and I remember clearly reading the Time–Life art books over and over, filled with beautiful pictures. Mom was a science teacher, so the whole world was a classroom for us, especially at our weekend house. The farm served as a natural learning site. Birding and following the plants of the season were always a big deal. When the trillium and dutchman's breeches bloomed, a celebration of sorts was in order. Because of this, we had reference books for plants and birds.

In first grade, we began to read. The first book I recall reading was the "Dick and Jane" book. When I started to put together that letters made words and could actually read them, I was really excited. Slowly, one word at a time, it all started making sense. In my mind, I could see Dick and Jane and follow them on their adventures.

In the summertime, we lived at the farm, and Dad would commute to the city every day. Once a week, Mom would take us to Thornville to wash our clothes at the laundromat. Liz and I loved laundry day. Mom would give us a dime, and we could buy some candy from the store across the street. The really big deal was that Thornville had a small library. We were allowed to go to the library, which was on the same block as the laundromat, and check out books. My library card, of which I was quite proud, was carefully put away after our visit.

Reading is a passport to worlds both magical and exciting. Through books, I can go anywhere, anytime, and visit created, rich, and vividly colorful worlds. Children inherently have vivid imaginations, and with books I could go anywhere.

Our school offered a program that I vaguely recall as being called "Scholastic Readers." A catalog was periodically offered, and we could order paperback books at what I assume was a reasonable price. I was allowed to buy as many books as I wanted. When the order came in, I would tote a full bag of books home, unlike other classmates.

THE GOLDEN INFANT
FORMULA ERA:
ALL THINGS CHANGE

An unpleasant, paranoid milk chemist living in a New York milk shed had a brilliant idea in the 1920s. Too many infants were dying from diarrhea and poor nutrition. Milk was unpasteurized. Breastfed babies did better. His idea was to modify cow's milk to make it similar to breast milk. Alfred Bosworth took his idea to the Boston Floating Hospital (an excursion boat that took infants out into Boston Harbor for the fresh air). He persuaded the chief to provide a small lab where he could experiment with differing formulations. Eventually he concocted a powdered formula with the approximate nutritional profile of breast milk.

Bosworth was afraid that someone would steal his idea, so he kept his secret lab notes on his person at all times. I interviewed him in 1956 for an article in *Pediatrics* detailing the history of the Boston Floating Hospital, including a description of his product.

He was a bitter and sullen old man. For a while he worked for the Moores & Ross Dietetic Laboratories, a small milk processing company in Columbus, Ohio, where a more refined formula eventually became Similac. He was so unpleasant and difficult that the company founders bought him out and sent him into retirement in Circleville, Ohio.

M & R struggled until the Second World War, when the company produced a gooey ice cream mix using butterfat that was not needed for infant formula. The navy bought the product to make off-shore ice cream on warships. Unused war profits piled up. When the war was over, the owners decided to expand the business by building a plant in Sturgis, Michigan, to make Similac powder. A second generation of family members took over, and a major marketing expansion began in the early 1950s. (I was in the first sales training class.)

At that time, most infants were fed diluted evaporated milk mixed with sugar (Dextri-Maltose) and then terminally sterilized. Breast feeding was out of favor. The times were ripe for a complete, nutritious infant formula to which only water need be added and sterilized. The idea fit the times. Pediatricians, general practitioners, obstetricians, and hospitals began to respond to our advertising and sales force promotion. Before long we were feeding over half the infants in the United States.

Other products were introduced: a liquid form of infant formula, a soy product, and several specialized products for sick or premature babies. The products were promoted only to physicians, never directly to mothers. We adamantly avoided direct consumer promotion, believing that it might interfere with the doctor-patient relationship.

Profits rolled in, and in 1964 we were acquired by the pharmaceutical firm Abbott Laboratories, which was then doing $136 million in sales annually. We became Abbott's cash cow, providing over 50 percent of its profits for many years.

A decision was made to expand into adult nutrition. Not wanting to confuse adult nutrition with the infant business, a distinct separation was made at the staff level. Two of the important products introduced there were Ensure, an adult nutritional supplement, and Glucerna, a slow-metabolizing supplement for diabetics. A product to compete with the sports drink Gatorade never got off the ground because promotional costs were so high, and the research required to prove product advantages was lacking.

Meanwhile, a new government program emerged that would change the momentum of the infant formula industry. In 1972, Senators Hubert Humphrey, Robert Dole, and George McGovern drafted a bill that provided indigent mothers with free infant formula for a year if they chose not to breast feed. It was entitled the Woman, Infants, and Children (WIC) program. The government bought formula at regular prices.

Because we had over half the market, our profits soared. Then a group of social activists proposed the idea that the companies selling infant formula should bid for the business and offer rebates per can. Those rebates escalated until in some cases it was not profitable to bid. The price per can was at or lower than our manufacturing cost.

The glory days of infant formula were over. Social activists belittled artificial feeding. Breastfeeding became avant-garde again, and evaporated milk formula no longer existed as a source of new business. Profits lagged, although division sales were now a billion dollars annually.

After my retirement in 1993, I wondered whether Abbott would sell off the Ross Division, since it was no longer the cash cow that it once was. The business measures I missed in my calculations were the rapid aging of the US population and overseas world markets for all nutritional products.

The adult nutritional market was an enigma to me because I never worked on that side of the business. Several imaginative people (such as Sue Finn and Jim McCall) wooed nursing homes and the dietetic profession to prescribe Ensure for their patients. The sales grew, but television promotion was never considered. It was too expensive and possibly in conflict with the pediatric business.

Now we see television ads for Ensure and Glucerna frequently with a brief mention of Abbott, but not of the Ross Division. Recently the corporation announced they were building a new plant in Ohio to produce adult nutritional products.

And it all started with an unhappy, paranoid milk chemist who was afraid someone would steal his ideas.

ANDY DOESN'T LIVE HERE ANYMORE

The President of our assisted living resident council came to our table to report that Andy was in the health center dying. Andy asked her to say hello to Jim and me. When she left, Jim and I looked at one another and said, "Who is Andy?" Neither of us could conjure up a vision of Andy or anything about him. The next day I asked Ann, who replied that Andy was the fellow in an electric scooter who ate at the second seating, as we did.

I came home and looked for someone named Andy in my telephone directory but could find no Andy or Andrew. At assisted living, we know one another primarily by our first names. Some residents might know last names, but not many do. Physical characteristics are more important: the woman with the loud sneeze is Ann, the lady with the pink walker is Gloria, etc.

Andy died, and his photo was displayed in the death nook. I recognized him immediately. (The death nook is a small alcove near the dining room. When a resident dies, his or her picture and a small bouquet of flowers appear.)

When Andy moved into assisted living, he lunched with us several times. Thereafter, we usually said hello to one another daily, but he took his meals at another table. He sold tires for a living—no, not automobile tires, but tires for large equipment that sometimes cost $13,000 each. After moving in, he acquired an electric scooter and had trouble driving. I wasn't aware that he was missing meals, nor did I know that he was so ill. Privacy laws prevent the staff from disclosing resident illnesses.

It occurred to me that many old folks just fade away, as Andy had faded away. We lose motor skills, memory, even old habits, usually slowly and bit by bit. Fading is a slow but inevitable aging process.

I am fading. I am four inches shorter than my full height. I notice that when I play computer mah jong, I sometimes can't find a match as fast as I once did and must use the "hint" function. Specific words and names are sometimes hard to come by.

I have a cousin whose husband is a devotee of generating family histories. He notes that burial records are often helpful in locating a deceased person. We intend to be cremated and have our ashes strewn on the Mendicino Coast and in Ohio. No records. We will just disappear back into the soil.

Not only did Andy fade away, but so did Helen Conant. When we lived in independent living, we played bridge with her every week or so. She was slightly frail but had a twinkle in her eye and was pleasant to be with. She had lived at Pajaro Dunes, an upscale resort development on the seacoast near Monterey, before moving in to our retirement community. She was widowed. Her husband was a prison warden and had been murdered many years ago. Her apartment had echoes of the seashore she loved with seashells, seaside paintings, and carved seabirds.

We stayed in touch by e-mail. Helen enjoyed a risqué joke, so we shared them weekly. I never saw her in the dining room and assumed that she ate at the first seating. Then she was gone, faded, disappeared.

Thinking about Andy, I wondered about Helen. Neither Marian nor I could remember her last name, so I called the other person with whom we had played bridge. She told me that Helen's son had moved her back to Pajaro Dunes and that she had Helen's son's cell phone number.

I called and learned that he moved Helen into his house in Santa Cruz with a full-time caretaker. "She has a window where she can look out at the ocean. She is frail but okay. She broke her hip a year ago. I'd let you talk with her, but she's getting ready for bed."

How satisfying to know that someone who had left my consciousness is there and available to chat. Our conversation, if we have one, will be simple and short. No long explanations needed.

Andy's last name may soon escape me. He faded fast, just as "Dialysis Jim" did.

ANOTHER SKILL FOR WHICH I WAS UNSUITED

During the years that I worked I was responsible for making four films: two training films for our salesmen, one film about education in Israel, and one film about women and infant care in Guatemala.

During the seventies we made a decision that Ross should make films to show sales trainees how to make sales calls. First we took an old basement cafeteria and turned it into a film studio. I hired a young man named Cliff to supervise the selection of needed equipment and facilities and then actually make films. From the beginning I noticed that Cliff had a characteristic that I didn't have—patience.

Filmmaking requires incredible patience. It is a horrendously ponderous procedure requiring details, details, details, plus elaborate planning and a willingness to do something over and over again until it is right. Those traits are the opposite of my personality.

Our first film was a training film shot at the Riverside Methodist Hospital in Columbus demonstrating a salesman calling on the newborn nursery where our product, Similac, was used to feed newborns. The film was narrated so the salesmen we selected would not have to talk, saving hours of audio set up. However, I quickly learned that hours of camera set up were required for every shot: lights, cables, and camera angles being rehearsed over and over, and then takes, retakes, and more retakes, until Cliff was satisfied he had suitable footage.

I had promised the hospital that we would not be intrusive or require much staff time, but I was very wrong. Some shots required hours of time, and I was helpless to speed things up.

Shooting a film is only the first step in the process. The film has to be edited, titles designed, script written, narrator and music selected, preliminary showings arranged with company executives, changes made, etc. It was unbearable. I felt I was living in a pit of dangerous snakes. That first film took many months to complete, but the end result was acceptable.

The next film we made was a film about manufacturing infant formula in our plant in Sturgis, Michigan. Our star was Dr. Jack Filer, our medical director. We had life-size flow charts designed by a convention display company in Cincinnati in front of which Jack would describe each step in manufacturing. We would then insert a clip of that actual process from the plant.

Milk processing plants have tile floors normally hosed daily with water for cleanliness. Yards of electrical cords on those floors was our first problem. Secondly, our powder product was dried in a huge room with three dryers several stories tall. Cliff set up every light we owned, opened the camera to maximum f- stop, but found he had nothing but dull, grim-looking footage. As a result, we cut in some colorful still photographs of those dryers.

During the time I was a fellow in the National Program for Educational Leadership, I was given a grant to make a film about the imaginative educational programs in Israel. (I have described that mess in another chapter entitled "I Shot the Mayor of Haifa.") What was planned to be a two-week shooting schedule turned into a three-day shoot with a surly camera crew. The film's title, *Israel's Second Line of Defense,* was meant to imply that after its war machine, education was highly valued and innovative. After viewing the completed film, a friend told me, "Interesting, if I only knew what it was about."

Returning to Ross after NPEL, I decided to make a film in a Third-World country that demonstrated women everywhere do the best they can to care for their babies, regardless of poverty or sordid conditions. I selected a Chicago firm to make the film and hired a well-connected Spanish-speaking liaison to interview poor mothers on camera. I visited the shoot in Guatemala twice during the filming and was distressed at how intrusive we had become. However, the finished product served us well with social critics and others trying to understand infant care in the Third World.

Back home, we realized that many business executives are not naturals in front of a camera. They often freeze, look uncomfortable, and resent being told that another take would be necessary. It didn't matter. Filmmaking was soon replaced by TV cameras with built-in sound. The results could be easily edited and cheaply made.

We closed the studio, let Cliff go, and returned to live training and off-campus plant visits for new salesmen.

I learned that filmmaking does not fit any part of my neurotic personality. I never want any more experience making movies.

"Quiet on the set! Action!" Phooey!

AT HOME WITH
MR. AND MRS. AND
MRS. AND MRS. BIN LADEN

"Dear, it's trash day. Don't forget to take the trash out to the curb."

"I told you a thousand times, we burn the trash. You never know who's snooping around."

"Okay, whatever."

So began the day of one of the most famous couples on earth. We wonder about the daily lives of famous celebrities. The Bin Ladens certainly are famous, but they have a problem. They are hiding in plain sight. To fool the police, the CIA, and the Pakistanis, they built a million-dollar gated complex down the street from the military academy and then sent out a message that they are very religious and should not be disturbed. They want no neighborly visits from the Welcome Wagon or anyone else, except maybe some neighborhood children to come in to play with little Osamas. (Each child who does come in is reportedly awarded a bunny as a gift. Finding a hutch of bunnies in Pakistan is no easy task.)

Security is the first priority of the Bin Laden compound. No telephones, no Internet, no Saturday trips to the grocery or department store. "I've told that courier a thousand times to leave his messages in the message cubbyhole we built into the wall. Park your car across the cabbage field, push back the marijuana plants, open the little pass-through, drop off the message, and leave promptly under cover of nightfall."

Family life is a bit complicated. Mr. Bin Laden has been married five times and has twenty children. His current Yemeni wife was a gift to him when she was fifteen years old. She has learned to be properly deferential to Osama. When the compound was constructed six years ago, Mr. Bin Laden agreed to build guest rooms to accommodate two former wives and assorted children. It is reliably reported that everyone gets along very well.

Did you see that bedroom? What a mess. That bed looked like it hadn't been made in years. Of course it had not been made in years. He's in it twice a day with the jar of petroleum jelly handy if needed. But none of the wives seem to tidy up the place.

Food! Hummus and bread for breakfast with a pot of cardamom-laced coffee. Lunch is the same. Dinner is hummus and some free-range chicken roasted in olive oil and garlic with bread for mopping. The chickens roam on the lawn. The Bin Laden children eat early. Osama and Amal eat after the children have been put to bed.

The daily routine varies according to the day of the week. The workday begins about ten in the morning. Osama goes to the situation room to be briefed on the news, the security report, the progress of the latest plot to blow up the Tokyo subway, and of course the latest soccer scores. On Friday, it's prayers all day long. Sunday is a regular workday: plots of terror, requests for funds, writing communiqués, television scripts, and more terror plots. Bin Laden never seems to tire.

The other day, little Osama came into the room carrying a tube of A Touch of Gray. "Daddy, I think you need to dye your beard. You are beginning to look old, and you are only fifty-four. A terrorist of your reputation should certainly have a black beard when filming." Actually, Dad doesn't care how he looks. He hasn't worn a disguise for six years. His problem is his height. It's hard to look five-foot-seven when you are six-foot-four.

As previously mentioned, security is the chief concern around the house. To anticipate an emergency, his wife sewed 500 euros into his shawl with two telephone numbers. You would expect that a MasterCard would also have been included, because 500 euros wouldn't buy a first class ticket to Brazil. With gas at $5 a gallon, only a small Vespa scooter would get him to the border. One of the telephone numbers was the cell phone of Pervez Musharraf, former Pakistani president, who promised to arrange safe passage out of the country. The other number was for the Pakistani spy service, disguise division.

After dinner, everyone settles in for a night of watching television on the new flat screen. The kids prefer *Sesame Street,* while Amal has a fondness for the house and garden channel, even though they don't employ a gardener any more. (The lawn has gone to hell.) Osama wants to watch himself on *Anderson Cooper 360* and *The Situation Room with Wolf Blitzer.* The collected crowd objects, and Osama storms off to his room to read pornography until Amal comes to bed.

After viewing the helter-skelter Bin Laden compound, we realize that Osama Bin Laden lacks the architectural sensitivity of Saddam Hussein, who knew how to build a show-off palace. Bin Laden must have known that he would be caught eventually. We suppose he didn't want to be seen as pretentious.

We never thought that for a moment.

He was just a regular, everyday terrorist who watched *Wheel of Fortune* and hoped for the best.

BOOK REVIEWS FOR THE TOGA TIMES

These brief book reviews were written for quarterly issues of the *Toga Times,* the internal newsletter of the Saratoga Retirement Community.

"OBAMA'S WARS"

by Bob Woodward, 380 pages.

Ever since Woodward and Bernstein wrote *All the President's Men*, Woodward has become the most respected "inside" journalist in Washington. His latest book purports to document the decision-making process by President Barack Obama and his National Security staff in planning for the Afghanistan war.

There are three reasons you should read this book:

1. Woodward writes with such authority that you feel you are inside the Situation Room with the principals. (And it's fun to peek.)

2. You will learn that making any decision in Washington is almost hopeless, given the

tension between the political and military advisors.

3. You will learn that Pakistan, not Afghanistan, is the hub of the trouble, particularly the al-Qaida safe zones.

This is not a brilliant read because too many cooks try to spoil the broth, but you won't regret reading *Obama's Wars*.

PARIS: THEY LOVED IT TOO

Since the time of Benjamin Franklin and Thomas Jefferson, Americans have found Paris an irresistible attraction. *The Greater Journey* by David McCullough goes back to the 1820s to detail the visits of Oliver Wendell Holmes, James Fenimore Cooper, Samuel Morse, James Whistler, John Singer Sergeant, Mary Cassatt, Harriet Beecher Stowe, Mark Twain, and others. They went to study art, medicine, architecture, and French, to work and to write. The sea voyage was long and dangerous, but within days they all thought it was worth it. Paris was charming and cheap, and the food was wonderful.

In the 1920s, F. Scott Fitzgerald, Ernest Hemingway, and George Gershwin made Paris popular again. This book will stir the memories of the many SRC residents who have visited there.

JUST WILD ABOUT HARRY TRUMAN

FDR died on April 12, 1945, and Harry Truman became president. Most of us were teenagers then and didn't keep up with politics. Truman was a farmer and politician of modest means from the Midwest, but he had qualities that would make him a remarkable president. He was honest and had a thoughtful temperament.

The Second World War was grinding into its fourth year when Truman learned of the A-bomb—after it was a fact. He had to decide whether to use it. He asked for data on how many American boys would die in an invasion of Japan and was told upwards of two hundred thousand. He dropped the bomb, and the war was over.

Thus began a presidency of enormous consequence: The Marshall Plan, Korea, the MacArthur firing, the Cold War, an electoral upset. He continued to be reviled by the Republicans, with frequent calls for his impeachment. His life in office was often a nightmare. Republicans were sure he would lose to Tom Dewey, but he traveled coast to coast by train, making hundreds of speeches, and won a full term because people loved his down-home approach.

David McCullough's book *Truman* is not a current best seller, but it was at one time. It is lavishly researched with a cohesive narrative that holds your attention for its 1,117 pages. A sure-fire read for eighty-year-olds.

The popular literature of the sixties was dominated by two authors, John Heller and Kurt Vonnegut. Heller wrote a loved anti-war story entitled *Catch-22*. Vonnegut wrote two books that captured the public's imagination, *Cat's Cradle* and *Slaughterhouse-Five*.

Catch-22 is set on an airbase in Italy during the Second World War. The hero has fulfilled all of his required bombing missions, but his commanding officer keeps increasing the number of missions required to be sent home. The situation is absurd as the story describes every possible army SNAFU. The hilarious book has lots of barracks talk, but you are old enough not to be too tainted.

Vonnegut's books are hard to describe. *Slaughterhouse-Five* tells of a captured American soldier who survived the bombing of Dresden, Germany, where 135,000 civilians were killed. Somehow, the hero, Billy Pilgram, ends up on a remote alien planet in a zoo where the aliens want to see him procreate. *Cat's Cradle* is a riff on science gone wrong when a chemical, Ice-Nine, freezes the earth. The action occurs on a remote island where atheist Vonnegut has invented a strange religion.

Both of these books reflect the mood of America in the 1960s, when things seemed to be coming apart.

A RIVETING READ

The Immortal Life of Henrietta Lacks by Rebecca Skloot was chosen by Amazon as the best book of 2010. It has been on the *New York Times* best-seller list for many months.

Henrietta Lacks was a poor, uneducated black woman who died of cervical cancer in 1951 at the age of thirty at Johns Hopkins Medical Center. The cells harvested from her have been used ever since for pharmaceutical research around the world. Author Skloot spent ten years tracking down the details and finding her five children, who feel they should be compensated.

"THINGS FALL APART"

More than fifty years ago, in 1958, Chinua Achebe wrote a novel about the arrival of British authorities and Christian missionaries in Nigeria in 1904. It was the first time a novel was written from the Nigerian point of view. The book sold five million copies all over the world, and the author was awarded more than twenty honorary degrees for his masterpiece.

The book tells the story of Okonkwo, a self-made man of the Ibo tribe. It describes Nigerian daily life in detail, with all its complexities. After an accidental shooting, Okonkwo, his wives, and his children are exiled to his mother's tribal home for seven years. By the time he returns, the British have established civil rule, and missionaries have built churches and schools. Even his son becomes a Christian convert, and Okonkwo realizes that things have changed but he cannot and commits suicide.

Although it is written in English, this short book conveys the Nigerian experience so brilliantly that the reader feels he or she is there.

AUTHOR CHRISTOPHER HITCHENS DIES

Christopher Hitchens died in December 2011 after a prolonged battle with cancer. Some among us won't give the contrarian's death a second thought. After all, he took on God, Mother Teresa, the Clintons, Kissinger, and others with wisecracks and despair.

Hitchens was a prolific writer and essayist in the grand, highly educated British style. He had a human side. He harbored Salman Rushdie for a few days when Rushdie was condemned to death with an Islamic fatwa. Hitchens was capable of changing his mind as new insights occurred to him.

We have three of his books in the SRC library. His most recent is entitled *Arguably,* a big book of essays that span the world in scope. Hitchens admired George Orwell as an essayist, and they share a common journalistic style and brilliant analysis. Hitchens's book *Why Orwell Matters* summarizes Orwell's style of essay writing and his place among the essay glitterati.

The third book is *Hitch-22,* a memoir filled with stories of his travels to dangerous lands and hobnobbing with famous writers, politicians, and assorted others.

Laced with high humor, insults, pedagogy, and wisdom, Hitchens will blow you away if you keep an open mind. *Arguably* is on the best-sellers shelf, and *Hitch-22* is in the biography section. *Why Orwell Matters* can be located on the politics shelf.

"THE HELP"

The Help by Kathryn Stockett has been on the *New York Times* bestseller list for nearly a year. (Putnam Press, 444 pages)

The novel takes place in Jackson, Mississippi, in the early sixties, when the civil rights movement is heating up. The matrons of the town have black maids to raise the children and to cook and clean their houses, but they don't let the help use their bathrooms for fear of disease. Most of the maids, on the other hand, have experienced decades of subservience and "know their place."

A young college graduate gets a job writing the helpful hints column in the local newspaper but needs a maid to tell her how to do things. That gives her the idea to write this book about how the maids feel about working in the white houses.

After Medgar Evers is killed, the frustrated maids agree to tell their side of the story, in spite of the many dangers of doing so. The eventual book is a sensation in Jackson. It will enlighten, entertain, and move you. It all feels real.

"Watergate", a novel by Thomas Mallon

Do you remember Martha Mitchell, probably drunk, calling the press and kvetching? Do you remember the eighteen-minute erasure on the Oval Office tapes by Rose Mary Woods? Do you remember John Dean telling President Nixon that "a cancer was growing"?

Thomas Mallon, an author who writes historical novels, has written a book that purports to tell us what happened behind closed doors during the biggest political scandal of our era. Mallon selects both famous and not-so-famous people to tell his story: Fred LaRue, assistant to John Mitchell, and Alice Roosevelt Longworth, ninety-year-old daughter of Teddy Roosevelt, who announces the "clock is dick-dick-dicking." Martha Mitchell blusters, and John Dean squeals to save his hide.

Some of the author's speculations stretch the imagination. He has Pat Nixon having a wealthy boyfriend who provides solace at critical times. The conversations at Washington cocktail parties titillate but are obviously fictional. But who cares? It's all fun and games.

Nixon was the only president to resign from office. The country was in crisis mode, but life goes on, and we recovered, probably with a few scars on the national ego.

The book is an easy and memorable read.

GO WEST YOUNG MAN:
I WENT

Everyone needs a little California in their lives. Raised in Philadelphia and oriented to the Atlantic Ocean, I had little expectation that I would ever go west, but fate intervened.

CAMP COOKE

Camp Cooke was located 9.2 miles north of Lompoc, California. It is now Vandenberg Air Force Base. The troop train that transported us from Maryland to California traveled west in the dead of winter. The windows were frosted, and we couldn't see out as we traversed the icy country. It was during the Korean War, and I was being shipped to basic training after being drafted in 1951.

Camp Cooke was a wilderness with acres of sandy soil, scrub brush, and intense blue skies. My platoon of recruits was comprised of several men who had graduated from college and were caught in the Korean draft. Several of us bonded, and when we began having weekend passes, we went out to dinner or thumbed rides to San Francisco. Other than being trucked to remote firing ranges, we did not appreciated the beauty of where we were stationed.

We knew the ocean was nearby, but had never seen it. After lunch one weekend, Roy McLeese and I decided to walk to the ocean across acres of firing ranges, sand dunes, and brush up to our waists. We made it, and when we saw the water, we felt like great explorers seeing the Pacific for the first time.

So began my love affair with California.

PALO ALTO

Unexpectedly, I received a job offer in the Palo Alto Unified School District in the early 1970s to manage long-range planning activity. I found a handsome but rundown house with four thousand square feet at the corner of Edgewood and Newell for $65,000. The house, a one-story in a horseshoe-shaped layout, needed paint and cleaning to make it into a fine home, the nicest home we ever had.

When we moved there, we did not know of Palo Alto's reputation. It was home of Stanford University, upscale boutiques, "culture" at every turn, gourmet restaurants—in short, the good California life just down the peninsula from San Francisco.

We learned to say, "Only in Palo Alto." For example, when the city employees went out on strike, I happened to walk by the picket line. A chamber quartet was playing classical music to soothe the picketers. The school district was performing in the high 90 percentiles on every measure but decided it needed a redesign. I asked a sixth grader what his favorite food was, and he answered "escargot." His father was an astrophysicist previously stationed in France. A sixth-grade field trip went to Hawaii to see the flora.

We drove to Napa for wine tasting. Along the highway, we stopped at the Heitz tasting room, then a seedy cinderblock building next to the road. I bought several bottles of cabernet for $12 a bottle (now they cost $60 or more a bottle). The wine was so big that overwhelmed every food we ever served it with.

We went to concerts, plays, and lectures, went whale watching, spent Xmas at Pajaro Dunes with friends, and toured Alcatraz. California was a heady experience, even though the kids discovered drugs and pot from Berkeley. Tensions always ran high. Marian worked at the Stanford Hospital, and I started cooking on weekends when she worked, bread and chicken supremes, for example.

THE SEA RANCH DIVERSION

Artist Keith Boyle told us about a recreational spot on the Mendocino Coast, a real estate development featuring one-of-a-kind cedar homes by famous San Francisco architects. The place was an old sheep farm ten miles long and high on a bluff above the Pacific Ocean. When it became time to move from Ohio, we wondered whether Sea Ranch might be a place to buy a retirement home.

We rented a house for six weeks and moved there during the middle of winter. It was the rainy season, and Route

One was washed out north and south of Sea Ranch. We were able to drive there only by a mountain ridge road.

We loved Sea Ranch. There were wood fires to supplement the heating system, misty mornings, rainy days, and grocery shopping in Gualala. Then reality struck. There was no sophisticated medical care nearby. We were in complete isolation, and it would have been a bad decision to live there. Subsequently we have rented houses at Sea Ranch for six or seven delightful weekends with friends and family, and intend to have our ashes scattered there.

A RETIREMENT COMMUNITY

When we lived in Palo Alto, we knew of a Presbyterian life-care community in Portola Valley, the Sequoias. We applied and were turned down; we had too many infirmities apparently. Janice continued to search and found a new retirement community being built in Saratoga, thirty minutes south of where she lived. We were accepted and have lived happily there since 2005 at the Saratoga Retirement Community.

The thirty-seven-acre campus at the foot of the Santa Cruz mountains was once an Odd Fellows retirement community. The old building was gutted and redesigned with cottages and apartment units added. Classy place.

Life was good for four years, and then Marian had a bad year in 2009—a serious fall or two, atrial fib, bouts of cellulitis, chronic cough, failed rotator cuff, etc. It was time to move to assisted living where our needs were cared for. While not quite as elegant as living in independent living, we are happy and comfortable, and our cat, Tillie, easily made the transition.

Marian volunteers in the company store, and I am the chair of the SRC Library Committee and serve on the resident council at assisted living. Our days are busy with doctor's appointments, meetings, and hours of reading and writing.

Today's date is December 11, 2011. Looking out our bedroom window at the trellis in the courtyard, I see pink roses in bloom—in December !

All people need some California in their lives.

COPING WITH THE FINALE

Last Friday, Marian's cough worsened. The cough came from deep in her chest. This had happened before, and it had developed into pneumonia. Her sputum was gooky, and that meant that a bacterial infection had begun. So we decided to go to urgent care to check it out at the Palo Alto Medical Foundation. Her lungs were clear, which meant no pneumonia.

At times like these, one inevitably thinks of what my daughter calls the "old man's friend" (pneumonia), which more often than not takes out eighty-year-olds. We will all leave this life, but most of us believe that would be inconvenient and ill-timed this year. We have appointments next week, and today we made plans for a birthday celebration in May. And I have a bit more writing to do before I finish volume three of my memoirs. But the grim reaper could arrive at any time. Let's face it—youth has fled. Middle age has past, and we are stuck in gimpy, geriatric bodies.

Several years ago we looked down from our second-floor apartment and saw a man lying flat on the pavement with a 911 crew applying CPR. Too late. He was dead. Then the police arrived, then the coroner, then the undertaker. It took several hours before the body was removed.

It provokes the thought of whether a sudden or a slow demise is preferable. The widow was surely in shock as she sat there watching the minions evaluating the corpse. A sudden death seems preferable to a long drawn out illness, as hard as that might be on the next of kin.

Are we ever ready? Some say they've had enough living and are ready to go peacefully. And in some cases death is merciful.

Death might be complicated. Coping with "heavenly hosts" might be a problem. Mothers, fathers, brothers, aunts, uncles, cousins, grandparents, friends, great-grandparents whom I have never met … how many generations will there be? Will Dad still be a chain smoker? Will mother still have Alzheimer's, or will everyone be healthy twenty-seven-year-olds? Or will everyone just be a benign "blithe spirit" and mind their own business? Marian will attest that I am rather solitary at home, don't talk much, prefer to listen to some classical music, work quietly at the computer, and think of things to write. Will small talk after death be necessary? Hope not.

And if hell is my fate, will I recognize anyone? It is not possible to relive life again and do everything right, never to err or sin. I did cheat on a Spanish test in high school once, but I think that would qualify as a minor infraction. What's done is done.

Many tombstones are inscribed with RIP, rest in peace. Eternal rest has a nice feel about it.

But today I have things to do.

RESPONSE TO COPING
WITH THE FINALE

By Janice Hudson

Someday you and Mom will pass away, and I dread that day. You and Mom are important to my life. The world will be an incredibly empty place without you.

But bodies just plain wear out. Somehow I think it's frightening that the older people get, the more complicated their medication schedule becomes. Add the inevitable loss of short-term memory, and it's a miracle most older folks don't inadvertently overdose on a regular basis. Insulin-dependent diabetics—Lord, how do they manage? Those teeny-tiny lines on an insulin syringe are hard to see. They have to change the dose with every blood sugar reading. With a tad of dementia or forgetfulness, an outrageous blunder with two different types of insulin could send blood sugars plummeting to zero.

Nurses call pneumonia "the old man's friend," not the "angel of death." Dying of pneumonia is easy. As the CO_2 level in the bloodstream rises, it acts as a narcotic. As it gets higher, one becomes unconscious but completely comfortable until the body just stops breathing.

So it's not a bad way to go. It also gives the family the chance to get used to the idea, unlike in a sudden death, such as a heart attack. A huge problem comes if some nitwit intubates the patient. There patients exist on a ventilator and eventually succumb to secondary infections, bedsores, and a host of horrible things.

Sometimes I was called to the ICU to intubate. If the patient was still awake, I would talk to them and tell them it would be unlikely they would ever get off the ventilator. If the patient was unconscious, I would talk to the family, who were often overwhelmed, and explained the deal to them. When they understood how uncomfortable an endotracheal tube is and that it wouldn't be coming out, they would often change their minds. It pisses me off that doctors tell the family that the patient needs to be intubated to "save their lives," when the only outcome is to die anyway, with a garden hose in their trachea.

So here's the rule: do not die in an ICU. Make sure there is an advance directive and everybody in the family is on board. It only takes one hysterical family member to say, "Oh please, save my _____'s life" to screw the whole thing up. You needn't worry about that, Dad. I won't let that happen.

We have a big problem in the developed world. We are managing chronic conditions too well, like diabetes. In the past people died much earlier from chronic diseases. Now they are living into their eighties or longer. You, Dad, are a perfect example of that.

Without Dianne Tallo (dad's Ohio internist), you would have certainly be gone by now. I thank her for that. This is sometimes good, as in your case, and sometimes bad. Imagine a demented incontinent person with no quality of life getting railroaded into intensive care medicine. This is one reason why my husband Mark hates his job so much. His unit is often filled with more or less corpses on ventilators who have Medicare/Medicaid. Our tax dollars are wasted because some idiotic family member cannot accept the inevitability of death.

Let's make a deal. You and Mom hang in there to at least your birthday—no, let's make it Mom's birthday. It would be a shame to miss a couple of days at Sea Ranch. As long as you and Mom stay out of the dementia party and can live relatively comfortably (meaning with only pain that is tolerable), stick around. Part of life is losing your parents—it's inevitable. But let me tell you one thing: it will suck.

DIRTY WORDS

George Carlin made a career out of a stand-up routine about the seven dirty words you can't say on television. If you want to know what they are, look them up on Google. I am too embarrassed to print them here. We are living at a time of permissiveness. That's okay by some but a matter of discomfort for others, namely me. I have heard all the words and have used some of them often enough. There are places where they seem natural: in the barracks, in locker rooms, in single-gender gatherings. What golfer has muffed a swing, and not said, "Oh shit!" And now I find that the f-word is scattered throughout most of the books I read. You might expect that in *Catch-22*, but not in a scholarly treatise entitled *Seven Days in the Art World* about the inner workings of the art market. Yet there it is.

Most of the censored words are references to sex, another subject that has been for some a matter of taboo, at least until the Woodstock era, when free love was condoned by many. The Victorians were hung up but often had wild private lives. The French kings had royal mistresses known to all. Queen Elizabeth I said "fart" on many occasions. Slowly, times have changed. Comedians on cable shows say many of the forbidden words all the time, and it's considered hilarious. (I reference Jon Stewart and Stephen Colbert.) Is this humor or therapy?

Yet every kid growing up has to be exposed to dirty words sooner or later with few holds barred, whether parents approve or not. Junior and senior high schools are the places where students learn about algebra and the seven dirty words, often in the same day. If you learn the words, you have to try them out eventually, don't you?

When we lived in Palo Alto in the seventies, I found my two children coming home with a colorful vocabulary, including that famous f-word, which was particularly disconcerting from the lips of my own teenage daughters.

Here's what I did at dinner one evening. "I'm finding that the language around here is getting too foul. I want you to know that your mother and I know these words, and I want you to stop using them here. Now, let's all say the word together six times aloud." And we did. F …, F …, F …," etc., six times. Marian looked at me ashen, but I had made my point. The kids understood, I think, and life went on.

I had a close friend who was a psychiatrist. We talked about prurience in the society. He commented that we require livid covers on gothic romances and bawdy talk in books because we are so messed up about sex education. If schools get too explicit, parents go wild, but how many of them have given their children an effective birds and bees talk? Not many.

Now we disguise the f-word. The kids say "freakin" this or that. But we know, don't we?

FLIRTING WITH
THE BIG APPLE

Soon after being discharged from the army, I was offered a job in the home office of M & R Dietetic Laboratories to write and teach promotional materials. In time I was included in the planning sessions at our New York advertising agency, William Douglas McAdams. Traveling to New York was a big deal for a naïve young executive. Mr. McAdams had died, and the president of the agency was Arthur M. Sackler. Artie was a psychiatrist who had supposedly isolated chemicals causing mental illness. He was the epitome of the wheeler-dealer but spouted endless brilliant ideas that made his meetings wonderful and mind boggling. His major accounts were Pfizer and Upjohn. He created *The Medical Tribune*, a daily newspaper for doctors into which all his clients placed their advertising at 17.65 percent commission. He had fingers in other drug magazines and companies. Reportedly he brought Valium, the tranquilizer, into the American market.

He was a noted art collector whose method was to pick an obscure area and then buy everything in that field until he cornered the market. Artie spent money lavishly, and he introduced we bumpkins from Ohio to the finest New York had to offer: restaurants, theater, night clubs, opera. Christmas gifts were lavish and imaginative; a

Rolex Oyster watch or a rare illustrated page from an ancient breviary are examples. His legacy is well known: the Sackler Gallery of Asian Art at the Smithsonian in Washington, the Sackler Gallery at the Metropolitan Museum in New York featuring the Dendur Egyptian Temple; and an art museum at Harvard in a building commissioned by British architect James Stirling.

Theater seats would always be in the first or second row center. We would be chaperoned by the current account executive. One AE was John Kallir, who had access to Rudolph Bing's box when Bing, the general manager, was not using it at the Metropolitan Opera.

After the theater we would visit a nightclub with the hottest acts: Edith Piaf, Errol Garner, Hildegarde, etc. At the time I did not appreciate what we were being treated to. I believed that we were being treated as all ad clients were.

Instead of returning home on the five o'clock plane to Columbus, I normally booked on the seven o'clock flight so that I could visit a museum or two after work or visit an art sales gallery to look at Matisses, Piccassos, Jackson Pollocks, and Van Goghs for sale. All were out of my price range as a salaried husband with a mortgage, a wife, and two daughters.

New York City presented me with a different vision of life. From time to time I would fly the helicopter from the skyscraper adjacent to Grand Central Terminal. Lifting off from the roof of the Pan Am building in a vibrating, noisy copter and looking down over the edge of the building created chills that I still remember.

Conversely, flying into New York at night over Manhattan was beautiful. In time the company rented an apartment at 55th and Lexington Avenue so that we didn't have to bother checking into varied hotels. My boss at the time, Jim Jeffries, and I were given four thousand dollars and told to furnish the studio apartment. We went to Bloomingdales and met a decorator in the furniture department who guided our choices. The place was tiny, but I always felt that I had my own pied-a-terre in the Big Apple.

How excitable and impressionable youth can be.

FORGOTTEN TURTLES

Woolworth's five and dime had an aquarium section in the back of the store where you could buy goldfish and small turtles. Mother never let us have a dog, but she would permit an occasional adventure with a small unobtrusive pet—a turtle.

The turtles on sale were the size of a silver dollar, green with a touch of scarlet on their heads. They were twenty-five cents each and probably infected with salmonella. The salesperson would put the turtle in a Chinese food carryout carton with a wire handle, and we would hurry home to create a house for our new guest. Mother kept an eight-inch goldfish bowl at ready for the arrival. A turtle was believed to live both in the water and on land, so a stone island was constructed in a half inch of water so he or she could sit up on dry land if he or she wanted to. (The sex of the turtle was nothing to be concerned about. I was eight or nine at the time.)

A new turtle came with new responsibilities: feeding, changing the water daily, and taking him or her for walk every day was an assumed chore. The box of food contained small pellets and came with an admonition not to overfeed the new pet.

For at least three days, the duties were performed flawlessly. Then boredom set in, and the beast would be abandoned. The water got cloudy, a peculiar odor arose from the bowl, and the hoped-for joy of ownership faded like an old bouquet. Miraculously, the bowl and the turtle disappeared. I never asked questions.

The same was true for the occasional pet goldfish. Goldfish cost a dime and were housed in the same eight-inch fishbowl. We might also buy a sprig of green plant. Oh, how I longed for a large aquarium with gravel, air pump, and a castle and bridge for the fish to swim around. But the same behavior ensued: overfeeding for a few days, a change of water once or twice, and then the dead remains floating on the surface a few days later.

Easter presented new opportunities for inappropriate pets. For several years running, we bought some baby chicks. The rule was they needed to be kept warm with a cardboard box for a home, some sawdust and sand for the bottom, and a saucer for water. For warmth, a light bulb was left burning above the box twenty-four-seven. They remained cared for for a week, and then the box started to reek, and parents would say it was time to take the chicks to a farm in the country. I was distressed by their disappearance, but the feeling never lingered very long. Wait until next year. (Stores sometimes sold chicks that were dyed blue, purple, red, or bright yellow. Our parents considered these too unnatural to purchase. Our chicks were unadulterated.)

Only once was a rabbit made a family member. It made funny little pellet turds that interested and amused us. It too disappeared before long. The rabbit was more a real pet than the others but was not destined to live in a box in my bedroom for long.

Every once in a while, in the spring, a robin fledgling would fall out of a nest and we would bring the poor bird home to raise. Out would come an eye dropper for feeding. Mother somehow knew the proper mixture to feed, and we would try for a few days. Then Mother would persuade me that Mrs. Robin was looking for her baby, and we would put the bird under a bush to await his or her mother's arrival. Needless to say the rescued "pet" was never seen again.

The naturalists and softhearted among us are saying, "No, no, no!" It is heartless to permit little children to have these sorts of abandoned pets knowing full well that they will come to a sad end. But isn't that true of all pets? What are pets for? To comfort, entertain, amuse, and bring happiness to the owner. All will perish eventually, many put down by an expensive vet. The humane society now charges $125 to put a cat down. The cat hospital in Saratoga charges $300. Inflation touches everything.

We permitted our children to have a box turtle named Pokey they saved from being run over by a car. He or she slept under Elizabeth's bed in a mattress box during the winter. The black snake, Louie, was captured for show-and-tell at their elementary school.

We didn't feed the snake. His fate was positive. A nearby farmer called to ask whether we had any black snakes on hand. He needed one to help control the mice in his barn. Off Louie went to a happy new occupation.

I feel better now.

GARDENS AND INEPT LANDSCAPE ARCHITECTS

My maternal grandparents lived in a two-story red brick home on the Lancaster Pike at the south city line of Lancaster, Pennsylvania. The house had a narrow, long, back yard of an acre that sloped sharply downhill. Grandad was an enthusiastic gardener. He terraced the property in order to grow flowers and vegetables. Halfway down on the south edge, he built a tool shed. As small children, we spent hours wandering the garden admiring the plants, playing, and exploring the musty tool shed.

My childhood home at 6433 Lebanon Avenue in Philadelphia had no garden, only a small dirt plot about two by four feet, adjacent to the steps leading to the front door. Every spring a very old man named Amos arrived and planted a bed of pansies for Mother. Otherwise, Mother and Dad had no interest in flowers or gardening.

When we moved to 7 Wiltshire Road in 1939, the new house was landscaped tastefully. A row of red azaleas flanked a small wall in the front yard. Several free-form beds contained ornamental shrubs, irises, and large rounded boulders for interest.

Dad loved roses. He bought a dozen and planted them against a six-foot wall at the back of the house in the shade. They never grew too well, but we nurtured their spindly growth. Dad was not a gardener.

Fast forward to the 1960s and the first house we bought in Columbus, Ohio. It had a small front yard and an ample backyard. I planted a row of lombardy poplars along the back fence, not understanding that they don't live very long. The poplars grew to twenty feet or so and promptly started dying . A small bed at the front of the house contained zinnias or some other common annuals we grew from seed.

In 1961 we bought the ninety-three-acre hill farm, and my life as a "gardener" emerged. The old farmhouse needed foundation plantings to supplement the old lilacs, forsythias, and flowering quince in the lawn. I bought holly, fir, and ivy and planted them too close to the house, causing radical pruning in too few years.

Later, several events necessitated the employment of a landscape architect to design major plantings. In 1978 we built a modern home on the side of a north-facing hill. The garden surrounding the house was planned to have nearly three quarters of an acre of perennials, flowers, and shrubs, all shaded by the woods to the south.

We hired Steve, who taught landscape architecture at Ohio State University. He talked a good game. I guess he thought I had unlimited funds. He insisted on building a three-dimensional topographical depiction of the entire ninety-three-acre farm before "conceptualizing" the garden. I soon learned that he knew design, but he didn't know plant stock. I asked for plantings of old-fashioned forest bluebells. When the bulbs came up in the spring, they were Spanish Scilla. We had lovely varieties of hostas and ferns mixed with flowers like coneflowers that bloomed most of the summer.

Don't ever plant a garden that large unless you have a professional gardener to care for it. Flowers must be deadheaded constantly, weeds invade whatever you plant, and in a year or so vigorous thinning becomes a necessity. I worked full time, so my weekends were taken up gardening in the summer heat. (Did I mention that we mowed five acres of grass?). A neighboring farmer, Cliff Noyes, with his wife and children, began helping me. We planted hundreds of daffodils and jonquils after some friends, Donn and Sharon, bought and planted a large bag of daffodil bulbs to remind the four of us of a May vacation and their marriage in Scotland.

I looked forward to frost and a fallow garden for the winter months.

Landscaper Steve disappeared when he received a commission for a major floral show in downtown Columbus. I did not miss him. At fifty dollars an hour, I couldn't afford him anymore.

When we bought the 1920 bank in the center of Glenford, Ohio, in the eighties, the sidewalks were cracked beyond repair, and there were no curbs nor any beds for planting flowers. I hired another landscape architect who promised me he was experienced enough to construct a sidewalk of pavers, build curbs, and plan a bed of day lilies where the septic tank was embedded. It was a disaster. He misjudged the slope of the lot, and the curb he planned was too tall at one end. The concrete he ordered was too wet, and the curbs started to disintegrate the day they were laid. Every finish date he gave me was delayed. I fired him after the mess he made. I was a demanding client, and he disliked me.

A few years later we bought three lots adjacent to the old bank. We could now plan a nice garden, with a lawn and shrubs beyond the guest house down the street. I selected yet another landscape architect. We liked his modest and tasteful design portfolio.

Several years later I had an idea to protect the setting of the bank. What Glenford needed was a small park in the center of town. My most recent landscape architect responded promptly, but with an elaborate plan that looked like Disneyland—walkways everywhere, high-maintenance flower beds, and other inappropriate features. We had a heart-to-heart conversation about his budget, which was three times higher than I had specified. We simplified everything drastically. The result was about right for the rural setting, and the flowering cherries he recommended delighted us each spring.

The great gardens of Europe require an army of workers. I was a gardener of one, until I had to hire an army of my own.

Now we live in a retirement community that is beautifully landscaped and well maintained by an army of workers. I like to think that the workers come free, but a significant percent of our substantial monthly rent goes to their upkeep. Gardens are an expensive luxury. Believe me !

HELLO, IT'S ME

Do you talk to yourself? I do. Actually, I talk to myself quite a bit. Some call it internal dialogue; others call it internal monologue. Whatever. All of us have that little voice talking in our heads most of the time.

Until I was forty, it never occurred to me that I should pay attention to that voice. Then I became a fellow in the National Program for Educational Leadership, a federal program to bring nontraditional persons into the school reform movement. A psychologist was assigned to me as an evaluator and as a counselor. During a talk-through session, I told Tom Milburn about the voice that seemed to chatter on as I go through life. Tom was intrigued, and he gathered the academic literature on internal conversation for me. He explained that that voice is an important part of the human condition. William James wrote about it decades ago. Whole books and many scientific articles have been written to describe it. The inner voice exists between the unconscious and the spoken word and is ever present.

Do you worry? Most of us do about all sorts of things. That little voice starts trying to solve the problem. "Do this; do that." These are emotional dry runs working through alternative solutions. For executives and leaders, worrying and listening to the voice is an important path to problem solving and planning out of the public eye. Some might call this intuition.

Are you creative? This ever-present voice is frequently a conduit between the entirely unconscious to the fully aware. How often have you said to yourself, "Where did that idea come from?" What a treat—ideas flow like spring water from an artesian well. Out pops a poem or story, and we hear it clearly, so clearly that we can say it or write it down.

Are you lonely? Well, you have a constant companion if you think about that way. After I studied this part of me that I had never explored before, I wrote a poem. It began, "When I am with me I am not alone." It's true. I can spend hours alone and never feel lonely. As a matter of fact, I like being alone, as my wife will attest. I always have company.

Complex little devils, aren't we?

HOSPITAL DAYS

What can be more mythic than a hospital? We are born there, and we die there, usually. To experience a hospital is an occasion to create memories, distant and recent.

Sometime in the mid-1930s, my mother had her appendix removed. The operation was performed in the old Jewish hospital on north Broad Street in Philadelphia. Children were not normally permitted to visit patient rooms, but it was arranged to let me go to the room briefly. It confused me. We were Presbyterian, and this was a "Jewish" hospital. It didn't compute. A friend of my father sent Mother a beautiful ten-inch blown-glass bowl enclosing a terrarium and a beautiful single orchid. That numbered and signed bowl (Steuben?) stayed in the family until it went to auction in the 1990s.

In my boyhood I had a terrible fear of ever having to go to a hospital. What if I was required to use a bedpan or a urinal? Fortunately my appendix never became inflamed, and my tonsils and adenoids never required removal, though I had many bouts of tonsillitis in those years. As a teenager I took pride in the fact that I never had been to a hospital.

Then in the 1990s the bottom fell out. Stroke, open-heart surgery, lung collapse, cellulitis, cataract removal, knee surgery—I became a regular hospital customer and an observer of hospital protocols, like checking vital signs at all hours, tasteless food, waiting for an MD to show up, blood drawing, housekeeping moving germs around, etc.

Then in January of 2012, a funny thing happened. My stomach started to churn, and I raced to the bathroom. Thus began a day to remember. A virulent norovirus had struck, and I was going down. At about noon a nurse stopped by and said, "We are sending you out. You fainted." She called 911, and a handsome group of Santa Clara emergency workers came to take my vital signs and prepare me for a gurney for a ride to El Camino Hospital, the new one.

I had on a t-shirt and pajama bottoms, no glasses, no shoes or stockings. I grabbed my wallet because it contained my list of medications, and away we went in the uncomfortable, bumpy ambulance.

The emergency room cubicles were self-contained rooms. The activity was fierce. Nurses, machines, technicians, and others created a flurry. All I remember is that I had the chills. Three heated blankets covered me like a mummy, but I was still cold. An IV was started. In an hour or so, they reported that my vital signs were all abnormal. My blood pressure was high, my blood glucose was four times too high, and my electrolytes were out of whack.

In time, an MD said they had decided to admit me, at least overnight.

After two days and perhaps eight bags of IV fluid, my electrolytes and vital signs returned to normal. On the third morning I was released, and my daughter came to retrieve me. But I didn't have any pants, underwear, shoes, or jacket. Discharging a naked patient seemed cruel, so they loaned me a pair of scrubs for pants, footies for socks, and daughter Janice brought a warm coat.

When we arrived home I was told that Marian and I were restricted to quarters and that our meals would be delivered. The fear, of course, was that we had norovirus, which can wreak havoc in retirement communities.

We were in jail for three days before being released to resume normal activities. Now we understand how a parolee feels.

Whoopee! Free to swing on a star again.

I WISH I WERE AN OSCAR MAYER WIENER

Everybody knows that a wiener is a hotdog. And every sixth-grade schoolboy knows that a wiener is a ... ahem, a p-e-n-i ... Oh, you know. For the last two weeks, the American media has gone nuts over the behavior of U.S. Representative Anthony Weiner. He has been caught sending photographs of himself in his tumescent underwear, bare-chested. These pictures were sent to women he had never met. Columnist Maureen Dowd claims he shaved his chest for the photographs.

This episode is sad. It is neither entertaining nor prurient. The man is obviously frozen in a teenage fantasy. One psychologist opined that the behavior is caused by a fear of aging. I think not. Somewhere along the way, Weiner's sexuality got sidetracked, and he is twelve again.

His wife is off traveling as Hillary Clinton's trusted aide. He was planning on running for mayor of New York next year. Both were on top of the world. Apparently, this Internet lark was somewhere beyond forty-seven-year-old Weiner's reasoning process. Or was it that he considered himself so untouchable (like Tiger Woods) that he thought any behavior was beyond reproach?

He has now resigned his seat in the Congress after a twenty-year career. Crisis managers say he could come back if he freely admits his guilt, takes steps to reform (two weeks of intensive therapy?), and lets a period of time go by during which he is unseen. That may be good advice, but will it really work? Even though this incident hardly qualifies as earthshaking, it will haunt Weiner for a very long time.

The media has had a field day. It was the lead story in most TV news shows we watched. The New York tabloids could not make their headlines more sordid. And all because of some irrational, dopey behavior. Forget the war in Afghanistan, the uprising in Syria, the Arizona wildfires. Weiner had all of our attention for the moment, his fifteen minutes of fame. Soon it will all be forgotten.

And then we will recall that Freud said: "Sometimes a wiener is just a hotdog."

OUR NATIONAL MEDIA – NOT

By Janice Hudson

Once upon a time, the "news" was truly news. I recall my father coming home to watch the evening news with Walter Cronkite. Journalism had truth—who, what, when, where, why. Journalists did not seem to have an agenda, right- or left-wing, and reported news that was pertinent that day. My family has included journalists for several generations, and I would like to think the "fourth estate" they represented were ethical.

I stopped watching the local evening news ten years ago. News programs became infotainment, and every local news program had a slant. Because I was in San Francisco, the news was always swinging to the left. Our talking heads fed us information that would garner ratings. I recall several stories that totally disgusted me. One was a man who had been shot by the police, and the story revolved around the grieving family. He was, of course, African American, and we got shots of his mother wailing, "He was always such a good boy," despite the fact that he had been in and out of prison for years. Then they zoomed in on his children—all from different women. This guy was not an upstanding young man—he was a gangsta covered with tattoos. The gist of the story was the police "jumped the gun" when he could have been subdued with non-violent force. So that means we get to send him to prison (where people truly learn to become criminals) on our dime.

The second story was about Code Pink in Berkeley. They were busy harassing a marine recruitment center. The war in Iraq was in full swing, and men were risking their lives and dying for our country. Of course, President Bush was considered Satan, despite the fact that the problems in the Middle East started back in the forties. Code Pink, where do you think we would be if we had not fought World War II? Remember Chamberlain and his efforts to appease Hitler?

The media has become a circus, and I don't trust any of the major news sources. As my father noted in his vignette, the spotlight was on some sick politician (aren't they all above reproach?) who decided to take pictures of his junk and posted it on the Internet. At the same time, the world is falling apart, the Middle East is even more dangerous after the overthrow of governments in Egypt, Libya, etc., and just who do you think is going to replace them? Most likely fanatics that will destablize the region even more. Our economy is headed down the tubes—the entire world economy, that is—which will have extremely grave consequences for every man woman and child in the world.

Every morning I open the San Francisco Chronicle and see what the media has dished up for the day. Mr. Weiner was huge news, and important stories are buried in world news, brief notes on some important event, without any who, why, where, or when. Even worse, all of the major news stories are coming from two or three major outlets. In a world where money can buy you almost anything, the "news" we are fed is calculated for its appeal.

It's sad to know there are really no trusted news outlets any longer. Last I checked, the Christian Science Monitor is one of the last standing sources that isn't biased. The Internet is a wonderful thing, except any crack head can write anything they want and people will believe it to be God's truth.

As horrible as this sounds, I don't pay much attention to "the news" any longer. Might as well check with the National Enquirer—the journalism standards are the same.

ISRAEL: THE DEFINITION OF COMPLICATED

Israel is the size of Vermont. Its size and influence on the world stage may be as important as China, Russia, and the United States. If Iran were to bomb Israel, it could begin a worldwide conflagration. Or if Israel bombs Iran to prevent the deploying of an atomic bomb, would the Middle East attack draw us into yet another war? Syria, Lebanon, and the Palestinians would revel in the opportunity to get rid of Israel.

Israel fascinates. A visit there is confusing. Underneath an air of normality, well-being, and enthusiasm is the smell of danger and unknowns. My first visit there was to make a film about the Israeli education system. The second visit was a tourist's guided ten-day tour, and my last visit was to visit Dr. Moussa Yodim, a well regarded investigator of the role of iron and dopamine in brain metabolism. In all three cases, we traveled from one end of the country to the other, marveling at the history, the unusual sights, and the diverse culture, but always with a subtle feeling of unease.

Religious diversity and tension are well known. The Wailing Wall, the Dome of the Rock, and the Church of the Holy Sepulcher are within blocks of one another in the old city of Jerusalem. Not only are the religions seemingly in opposition with one another, but there are serious arguments within denominations and sects.

Many years ago the two-lane road from Jerusalem wound down through bleak, uninhabited mountainous desert to the Dead Sea. Now we observe Israeli settlements on hill tops with electric and water pipes servicing them on the bare ground. Anyone with a small explosive could cut off an entire community.

But life goes on as if there were no problems. Arabs and Jews haggle over prices in the little shops in the Old City of Jerusalem. We bought a sheepskin jacket for my daughter. The asking price was eighteen dollars, what I thought was reasonable. My Israeli friend David Nevo said no, it would be an affront to the shopkeeper if we didn't haggle. He took over the bargaining, and the coat sold for ten dollars.

I took two American friends to the Church of the Holy Sepulcher. They were wearing shorts. They were told they must wear long pants for admission. A "salesman" took them to a room nearby and fitted them out with rented pants to wear over their shorts for ten dollars each.

Israel presents all manner of delightful things to see and do. To the north lies Ein Hod, a town devoted entirely to art. Year after year people go there to create or buy art. (The community even has a web site.) The town of Safed also had an active art colony. I rue the day that I didn't buy a gigantic, six-foot iron grasshopper attached to the side of a building. You could also buy huge iron spiders, praying mantises, and bees. Why? Because they were delightful.

At the north end of the Sea of Galilee lies the remains of the ancient town of Capernum, said to be the home of Peter and site of much of Jesus's ministry. The place is a few acres in size next to the water. A monastery welcomes you at the gate. Inside are the ancient remains of a synagogue and a Christian church. The dig revealing the remains of a house said to be Peter's is now glassed over for preservation. The entire setting is in a quiet, rural countryside. Next to the ruins a Bedouin grazes his sheep near his tent.

Back in Tel Aviv, the Hilton Hotel lobby buzzes with lunchtime diners. I have never seen so many cell phones in my life. It seemed that every person had a cell phone in his or her ear jabbering away, doing the nation's business. All in all, a visit to Israel is like a psychedelic trip. It leaves one in a state of awe.

At the end of the seder meal, the celebrant says, "Next year in Jerusalem." Israel may be the center of the Jewish universe, but it remains a troubled place. Let's hope there will be a next year.

BOTH LIBERAL AND CONSERVATIVE

Whoever said that people had to be consistent? Most people are a little bit of this and a little bit of that, and so am I.

Many years ago I was asked to serve on the Planned Parenthood Board in Columbus, Ohio. At that time, the focus of Planned Parenthood was contraception. Birth control pills were being introduced, and one of the programs we developed was entitled "Pills for the Hills." It was designed to provide contraception methods for rural women in the Appalachian foothills.

The chairman of the board was a woman named Babs Sirak. Her husband was a surgeon, and they represented the most liberal and most Democratic family in the city. Babs had earrings made from intrauterine devices. She wore them to most board meetings and to other social events. I marveled at her ease with matters sexual. She was the daughter of the woman who started Planned Parenthood in Columbus. If abortions were being performed at the facility, I was unaware of it.

How do I feel about all this in 2012? I believe we have too many people to care for properly on earth, especially in most urban settings. So I am by nature pro-choice. As a society we are truly messed up about procreation and sexuality. Children often giggle when they find out where babies come from. Inhibitions lead to all manner of abuse, including the elementary school teacher in Los Angeles having his blindfolded students taste his semen.

Several years after serving on the session, I was asked by my Presbyterian pastor to head up a new committee he called Religion and Race. Our church was entirely white with the exception of one black soprano who sang in the choir. (Later she became the first black member.)

I started reading black literature, paid attention to the unfolding civil rights movement in the South, joined an all-black leadership conference modeled on the Southern Christian Leadership Conference, and became the chair of the Presbytery committee on Religion and Race representing nineteen churches. Personally I began to make friends with a number of black spokesmen and invited them to spend weekends with us at the farm.

Both my work in civil rights and with Planned Parenthood might give you impression that I was liberal, but I was not and am not. I am suspicious of government intervention; I have voted Republican all my life. I abhor the national debt we have inflicted on our children and grandchildren. In short, I am a grumpy conservative.

For example, two government programs irritate me, one federal, and one state sponsored.

Both Marian and I have trouble walking. No big deal. The TV ad says that electric scooters will make our lives easier AT NO COST. Medicare provides them. All you need is a doctor's prescription, and the thousand-dollar scooter comes free. Great! But no one ever asked whether we could afford to buy Marian's scooter. We could, but didn't. Shame on us.

My electric scooter came from an estate sale. It's a two-thousand-dollar scooter my daughter bought used for three hundred dollars. I wonder how many "free" usable scooters are sitting in garages gathering dust and grime. Thousands, I suspect.

Once a week I see a television ad for a program in debt-plagued California to enhance disabled hearing persons use of telephones. The ad proclaims that the state can provide phones with large numbers, phones with loud speakers—just call this number. Is there a means test? I doubt it. I can buy my own damn phone. I'm steamed.

Do I care that people with bad hearing or sight should be helped? Of course they should, but we must live within our income, set priorities, behave realistically. Too many governments just spend thoughtlessly on every good idea that comes along.

Therefore, I am socially liberal and fiscally and privately conservative.

But I don't go to tea parties.

MARIAN GOES SHELLING ON SANIBEL

Destiny or chance? Probably chance.

The director of market research where I worked, Gil Martinez, had been invited by a friend to share a vacation on Sanibel, the small barrier island off the coast of Ft. Myers, Florida. Gil liked the place and bought a two-week timeshare condo on the Gulf of Mexico near the lighthouse on the quiet end of the island.

A year or so later, he did the same for us, inviting Marian and me to visit this place famous for its shelling and low-key ambience. It was wonderful, and we decided to buy a timeshare at the same location. After we signed the papers, the seller backed out, and I was storming mad.

We walked across the road to the Lighthouse Resort and Club, asking whether they had anything for sale. They did. Unit 304 was occupied by a family who had "aged out" and were selling. The unit was the third-floor corner unit directly on the bay, with views of the ocean on the right, and far away, the causeway separating the mainland from the island. We bought it immediately and were eventually able to buy the entire month of January in the same unit. And so began nearly two decades of vacations. I had a two-week vacation, but we thought our children and friends might enjoy vacationing there.

The well-maintained unit had three bedrooms, washer and dryer, dining room, and three balconies, one screened in—a total of 2,800 square feet. We felt blessed.

Because of a combination of prevailing winds, tides, and location, Sanibel is best known as a shelling mecca. Most travel brochures feature the "Sanibel stoop," people bending over looking for a new find in the sand. In the first year of looking, most people search for big, colorful, and recognizable shells. Thereafter, the pros look for a myriad of small shells, many the size of your little fingernail.

Marian enjoyed getting up early before the beaches were picked over. If she was not in the apartment when I woke, I might spot her in a yellow windbreaker combing the beach in front of the condo. (Raymond Burr, who portrayed Perry Mason, funded a shell museum on the island.)

Five thousand marshy acres on Sanibel are dedicated to the Ding Darling National Wildlife Preserve, home in the winter to flocks of white pelicans, roseate spoonbills, and other exotic waterfowl. At least once a week we drove the one-way dike road through the marshes searching for new birds.

Alligators are everywhere on the island, but one lone crocodile swam into Ding Darling and became one of the most famous tourist attractions in the preserve.

A naturalist, "Bird" Westall, who later became mayor of Sanibel, introduced dozens of tall breeding platforms to the island to attract ospreys. Most mornings you can watch an osprey (sometimes called a sea hawk) hunting for fish, swirling over head, and diving from a hundred feet in the air to grab a fish in his talons.

Dolphins swam by in late afternoon with a slow undulating stride that intrigues and pleases.

While we ate most meals at home, we frequented many of the cafes and restaurants dotting the island. Our luncheon favorite was the Mucky Duck on the adjoining island of Captiva. An ersatz British pub, the trick was to get a table by the windows. If you were disappointed, the maitre d' would roll over a window frame on a dolly, thus giving you a table "by the window." The nearby Bubble Room served outrageously large food portions presented by waiters in Boy Scout uniforms.

Sanibel adheres to a strict building code. No buildings are permitted over three stories, so there are no high rises. The main road up and down the island has no red lights. Before a hurricane, Australian pines covered Periwinkle Drive. Driving felt as if you were going through a green tunnel. However, the winds blew over many of these shallow-rooted trees, and now sunlight covers the road.

The library provided the computer facilities we needed to check and send e-mail, and borrow books or video tapes. In this setting we were never bored and always were sorry to leave to go back to the dreaded Ohio winter.

After my stroke in Ohio, a neighbor, Norm McCray, drove us to and from Sanibel, making the trip in two days. What a treat to leave frosty Ohio and feel the air change to tropical as we entered Florida.

After we moved to California, we went back to Sanibel once. Norm drove us home across that unending Interstate 10 across Texas. We've now sold weeks one and four but retain weeks two and three in case family or friends might like to use the condo.

Do we miss Sanibel? Yes, very much.

MASSAGE:
"YOU'RE IN GOOD HANDS"

From time to time, the president of Ross Laboratories would take his cabinet on a retreat, usually to a nice vacation spot for two or three days. We planned such a retreat to the Greenbrier, the famous hotel in White Sulphur Springs, West Virginia. A week or so before the trip, Abbott corporate headquarters called and told us to cancel the meeting for financial reasons. The hotel refused to refund our prepayment, but would honor our ten-thousand-dollar credit whenever we could come.

Six months later, the "go" signal was given, and about ten of us drove to the hotel.

The usual pattern of work was a five-hour business session followed by an hour or so of recreation before dinner. Greenbrier has several famous golf courses, and some in our group hit the links. Some went skeet shooting, and a few of us decided to have one of the spa treatments offered: massage.

I had never had a massage and reasoned that my life would not be complete until I added this to my life experiences. The spa at the Greenbrier is famous.

We were assigned to a small undressing room and given a bathrobe to wear when we shed our clothes. The first phase was the bath. The bathtub was extra deep as we slipped into the soothing warm water. Candles were burning on the edge of the tub, and soft music played in the distance. I think the bath lasted twenty or thirty minutes before we were taken to the scotch shower.

What is a scotch shower, you ask? It is a sort of closet with a gaggle of shower heads coming from above and from all sides except the front. There a staff member was stationed with a large hose, like a fire hose. At the appointed time, I was told to put my hands over my private parts, and the water poured down and from the sides. The hose was pointed directly at me, shooshing with considerable force on my chest. A few moments later the warm water suddenly turned cold, and I was sprayed with what I classified to be ice water. Seriously, I thought that I was being tortured in some upscale way. Fifteen minutes later, after being thoroughly hosed, I was directed to the massage parlor.

Naked, I was placed face down on a waist-high table with an itty bitty towel over my backside and lathered with a scented oil. The masseuse assured me that when he finished I would float on air. Okay, I thought, but did I mention that I am ticklish? I had seen many massage scenes in the movies with different types of rubbing or pounding. This man's technique was deep rubbing with the palm of his hand. From time to time, he would comment on my supple back or my well-muscled legs. But when he got to the bottom of my feet, he started grinding them with his knuckles. That did it. The discomfort was worse than pain, and I asked him to back off that tactic. It seemed to me that he was taking too much time trying to locate my tense spots. It was an hour-long massage. Fifteen minutes would have been too much.

My mind floated to the question of a career consisting of standing in a dark room for years running your hands over 98 percent of men's nude bodies eight hours a day. I guess someone has to do it.

Following the massage, we were escorted to a small room with a comfortable bed. I was wrapped tightly in a sheet, the lights dimmed, and I assumed I was to take a nap. I don't remember nodding off. After a half hour, someone turned on the lights and handed me my clothes

Going to the Greenbrier was supposed to be a special treat. The restaurants were luxe, with a wandering violin player and children dressed in coats, ties, or expensive dresses. The food was excellent. I am glad that our credit permitted us to have our retreat there, but I have no desire to go there again, either for a massage or anything else. The hotel seems suited best for grand dames with real pearls and rich husbands who want to golf all day.

And I do not long for another massage (unless, of course, it qualifies as exercise).

MASSAGE AND MUDBATHS IN CALISTOGA

By Janice Hudson

My father is nuts. To me, a day at the spa is delightful. A masseuse with good hands can melt me into butter, calm my brain, and soothe tense muscles. The Monster (MS) has a horrible trick up his sleeve. He causes all my muscles to spasm, sometimes to tetany, which can be horribly painful. Massage is one of the tricks I have to thwart the pain.

Earlier in my life, I loved going to Calistoga, California, located at the north end of Napa Valley and is famous for its mud baths. Allow me to explain the process.

You are lead into the spa to disrobe. An attendant softly knocks on your door and then escorts you to a large room with concrete tubs filled with hot mud above a hot spring. With a board, you are gently rolled into this mud, which is somewhere around 110 degrees. Your neck is placed on a pillow, and the thick, warm mud is literally shoveled onto your body. And yes, the "down below stuff" sinks down into ooze as well. Takes a bit to get used to that.

The feeling at first is rather odd (it is mud, after all), but then it becomes quite comfortable and relaxing. Fifteen minutes is about all I could ever take. Then you are rather ungracefully pulled out. I realized after my second mud bath it's akin to very hot quick sand.

Once freed from the mud, they lead you to a shower where the mud is scraped off, including the privates. Then you are led to a wonderfully cool bath with cool washcloths laid on your forehead. This is followed by a massage.

I prefer to think of mudbaths as a complete body mud mask. Betcha you'd never do that, huh, Dad?

VERNON'S LAKE

In truth, it was never a lake. It was a farm pond. In 1961, Marian and I bought an old hill farm in Perry County, Ohio, for a weekend retreat. We paid $11,000 for 93 acres and house with several oil and gas wells. Mrs. Torbert held the deed, and we paid her $75 a month. The one-hundred-year-old farmhouse was made of solid oak with poplar siding. It had three bedrooms upstairs, a parlor and a living room, a dining room with a potbellied gas-converted stove, a kitchen, and a dirt basement.

The house was sited on the side of a hill. A magnificent white oak tree grew below in a ravine with a runoff from a spring that ran hard all year. After moving in, we began talking about whether it might be a site for a farm pond for swimming and other water activities. We called Vernon Mack, a farmer who also had a bulldozing business, to make an assessment. He thought the job might be done.

The first task was to fell the white oak tree. Vernon set dynamite under the tree, and we watched as it blew two feet into the air and settled back down. Next came tires to set a fire to burn the gigantic roots. I remember fire and smoldering for a week before he wedged the huge root remains into a position to be known as the filter dam opposite what would become the main dam. The pond would contain the surface drainage of 54 acres, and the filter dam was necessary to contain the silt of those acres. Then the scraping began. The pond would be 19 feet deep at its deepest point. The big dam took shape, perhaps 150 feet across at the top, with a one-foot corrugated overflow pipe 6 feet below the top of the dam. All in all, the pond was about 3/4 acre when filled.

One further feature we insisted on was a sanded swimming shelf for the kids to wade and learn to swim in. We also sanded a beach for the girls to play. Vernon seeded the surrounding raw dirt with rye grass, and we waited for winter and the pond to fill. By February it was full but very muddy.

In the spring we began to learn about pond management. We used copper sulfate to kill the algae, and later, chemicals to kill the grassy undergrowth. Then we were off to the Buckeye Lake fish hatchery for largemouth bass and bluegills. They were an inch long when we put them in. How great could life get?

By the second spring, we were ready for full use of the pond, mostly for swimming. The spring-fed pond was too cold for me to enjoy, except in July when it finally warmed up. Our friends the Behns bought us a aluminum rowboat that we christened *Maid Marian*. I searched the shores for life and found all manner of beasts: frogs of all sizes, snapping turtles, muskrats, and once even a beaver.

We had a dedication ceremony and invited the neighbors. I had a sign painted that read, "VERNON'S LAKE no trespassing allowed." The space was too large to fence in, and I was afraid of "attractive nuisance" legal problems. Eventually we allowed neighborhood farmers and kids to fish, but I remained wary.

After three years we were spending seven hundred dollars a year on chemicals that bothered all of my sensibilities. Were the chemicals doing any harm to the children? Was the runoff affecting the stream below? We heard about weed-eating, sterile triploid carp from the county farm agent, and we ordered a few. Marian claimed that they must have exited through the pipe, so we looked for a new source at a private hatchery about twenty miles north of Newark. This time the fish were over a foot in length. They started eating the weeds, and grew to enormous size. They liked to sun themselves near the surface and looked like a fleet of submarines, but the pond was almost weed free.

Fred Behn built a float where we could sun or have picnics in the center of the lake. One night we decided to eat by candlelight on the float, but Bob Dutton moved suddenly and our good brass candlesticks sunk to the bottom, never to be retrieved.

I calculated that the cost of the pond was about the cost of a Volkswagen. It gave us years of pleasure, including in the winter when it froze and we could ice skate or sled on it.

Other tales could be told, including the night we all decided to go skinny dipping after a dinner party. It was pitch black—until someone turned on the floodlights, which caused a mad run for towels.

Too much wine will do that to you.

MEMORIES OF THE LAKE

Turtles, Trees, Rowboats, Snakes, and a Dog
By Janice Hudson

My parents didn't believe in corporal punishment, with two exceptions:

1. Going into the street alone

2. Going into the lake without an adult

Therefore, I was spanked twice. The pebbles at the curb of our home were too enticing, and I just wanted to look at the fish in the shallow area of the pond. I swear only one toe was in the water. Well, maybe a little more than that. Mom came running down to the lake, yelling. A small piece of me hoped (okay, I admit it, both of my feet were in the water up to my ankles) that she would merely yell at me. Nope.

Dad and I were recently discussing the lake. He said, "It was the best seven hundred dollars I ever spent." He stocked the pond with largemouth bass and bluegills as food for the bass.

The first time I took my husband, Mark, to the farm, he got up early on a rainy morning to fish. About seven that morning, he came running into the bedroom. I was still happily asleep, warm and comfy under the covers. "Look!" he yelled, dangling an enormous smelly bass, dripping fish goo and water onto my face. "Can you believe the size of this thing?"

Yes, it was huge. I had fished the lake for years, but being awakened with a wet bass wasn't my idea of a romantic morning awakening. "I have never in my life, ever, caught a bass this size. Hon, you should have seen how it fought! Good God, this thing is a monster. Look, honey! Isn't this incredible?"

"Wow, that thing is huge honey," I said, trying to move away from the dripping water. "But could you back up a tad so it's not dripping in my face?"

Many local farmers fished our lake, usually with simple, long bamboo poles. When I was really young, I saw them pulling out big fish. I fished that pond for years. One afternoon, I was casting for bass. Something huge took the hook. Like a pro, I wrestled it in. An ominous snapping turtle came flying out of the lake. I threw my pole down and ran.

In the summer, Mom, Liz, and I lived at the farm, while Dad commuted to Columbus to work. Liz and I always begged to go swimming, but we could only go if Mom was there to watch or swim with us. We bugged her to finish whatever she was doing so we could swim. In the meantime, Liz and I wandered the woods, knowing every square foot of the farm. When Mother was finally ready, we'd run down the hill and hit the water with a fierce splash. Those days spent swimming with Mom are some of our happiest memories of the farm.

Our parents often swam with us, and Mom would let us ride on her back in deeper water until we became competent swimmers. Sometimes she would carry us to "the point," a corner of the lake way across. She taught us how to hold our breath under water by standing in the shallow area (which had a sandy bottom), and we would pull ourselves around her legs in a figure eight. With Mom as our teacher, we learned how to hold our breath and not be afraid of putting our heads under water.

She enrolled us in swimming lessons in Thornville, a nearby town with a public pool. All I remember was the water was exceedingly cold, and we believed they dumped ice cubes prior to our arrival. My first lesson was an insult. My sister went into the intermediate group, but I was assigned to the baby group. "Okay, kids, hold your nose and put your head under the water." Since Mom had already taught me to hold my breath; my indignity was intense.

At the far end of Vernon's Lake were three enormous maple trees. My birthday, October 25, almost always fell on the week that the trees were at the peak of their fall colors. One was red, another orange, and the third yellow. To the right of the pond was a hill filled with beech and other trees, so the large colorful maples were surrounded by the varied colors of other trees. Who needs to go to Vermont to be tree peepers? Just come to the lake.

Tuni, aka Petunia Daffodil Flower McCollough (forgive me, I was only seven), was my mongrel dog that we had picked out of the pound. Some would describe her as funny lookin'. The most distinguishing part of her body was her tail, which curled around itself in tight circles. Among her hobbies were swimming and fishing. We'd find her in the shallow area watching the fingerlings intently. Suddenly she would pounce, trying to capture a fish under her paw. To her frustration, she never did learn the coordination of putting her head underwater and picking up her paw to grab a fish. During their hatching season, bluegills made nests in a shallow muddy area, dozens of round nests with bluegills swimming fiercely in circles to ward off intruders—such as Tuni. She would stand in the middle of them, her head swinging from side to side, picking a target. She gave it up when she was attacked and nipped.

The Behns, good friends of the family, bought Mother an aluminum rowboat for her birthday that was christened Maid Marian. We often cruised aimlessly around the lake with Tuni as the bowsprit. When she tired of rowing around, she would jump out, no matter how far from shore we were, and swim home.

For fun we turned the boat over and swam underneath. There was an air pocket to poke your head up into. It was quiet, cool, and from there we could look down and watch the fish below.

Two springs fed the lake. One was just below the farmhouse and was the source of the water for the house before a deep well was dug. Very large boulders covered with soft green moss marked the place where water emerged from the hill. Over the years the boulders had become unstable. Mom wouldn't let us go into the cool pool of water fearing the rocks might collapse. The other spring came off the hill on the other side of the lake. It was gorgeous, and there was a small waterfall cascading down some large rocks. Liz and I played there. One day we really screwed up.

Liz and I often caught harmless black snakes. We would keep them for a week, take them to show and tell, and then free them into the weeds. We were playing in the gushing spring when we spied a snake. We ran to the house to grab the snake cage, but this guy was a tad different. As we put the cage over him and closed the door, instead of sitting quietly, he was striking the edge of the cage. Snakes usually smell kind of nasty, but this one really stank. No matter. We ran back to the house to show Mom our new catch.

She looked, her eyes narrowed, her face reddening. "Girls, what have I taught you about poisonous snakes? What kind of heads do they have?"

"Uh, triangular," we replied, studying our toes.

"And what shape is his head?"

"Mmmm, triangular?" we offered.

"And what shape are pupils?" she demanded.

"Uh, round," we replied.

"And exactly what are the shape of this snake's pupils?" she asked.

"Uh, slits," We realized we were in big trouble.

"Do you think this is a black snake?" she demanded as the snake bit the cage again, venom dripping from his fangs.

"Uh, guess probably not," we admitted. In our excitement, we had managed to catch a water moccasin, one of only three types of venomous snakes in Ohio.

As Dad said, the pond was the best seven hundred dollars he ever spent. I agree.

USELESS MIDDLE NAMES

Parts of us are unnecessary: a primitive tail, a useless appendix, and most of all a middle name. All cultures have their own traditions about them, some more elaborate than others. Prince William got a bunch. He is officially William Arthur Philip Louis Mountbatten-Windsor. That's more middle names than he can usefully use. In America most people only use a middle initial for official use. Mine is "D."

D stands for Dudley, and I warn you not to kid me about it. I've never liked it. Remember Dudley Do-Right? "Dudley" doesn't have much savoir faire to commend it. My father told me I was named after a newspaper reporter he once worked with, Tom Dudley. I Googled the name and came up with two Tom Dudleys. The first was a governor of the Massachusetts Bay Colony in 1629, and the second manufactured bathroom equipment. So I finish my life never really knowing from whence Dudley has sprung.

Even our daughter's middle names have obscure sources. Daughter Elizabeth's middle name is Lynn. We selected that name for a special reason. My wife's first name is Marian; her mother's name was Marian. When the phone rang at their family home and someone asked for Marian there followed the question, "Which Marian do you mean?" We decided that another generation of Marians would be one too many. When Tish was born, I had the unenviable task of calling Grandmother.

"It's a little girl, and mother and baby are fine," I said.

"What is the baby's name?" the new grandma asked.

"We plan to call her Elizabeth Lynn."

There was a long silence on the other end of the line. "Where did that come from?"

From that moment on, I think Big Marian discounted me as not worthy of her daughter.

Our second daughter is Janice Dodge McCollough. The first name is easy to explain. Marian's closest friend was Janice Alexander, and we both liked the name Janice. As for Dodge, the answer is remote. Marian's father's mother was born in Dodge City when the West was still wild and hangings common. Her name was Mary Dodge Brown. Hence, Dodge was chosen to include Janice's great-grandmother.

My wife's middle name is Matilda. That was a great-grandmother's name, a rationale for that moniker.

If your name is John Smith, I suppose that a distinguished middle name might have some value. J. Ferdinand Smith does have a distinguished ring about it.

We eat meals with a retiree whose firstborn son was sired in Japan. To celebrate the birth, the middle name Miomotomasachi was appended. The cause? Three martinis or an overabundance of sake. Alcohol had something to do with my father's middle name. Dad became Huston, a misspelled Houston. Grandfather declared he was drunk when he signed the birth certificate.

What's your middle name? We won't tell.

TOM THE PSEUDOARCHITECT

The other day someone asked, "If you had to do it over again, what would you like to do for a living?" Without hesitation I answered, "Be an architect." History provides many examples of laymen having success at designing things, notably their houses: Thomas Jefferson at Monticello, and George Washington at Mount Vernon. When we built a new house in the mid–'70s on the farm, I had the pleasure of designing it myself.

I knew a Frank Lloyd Wright-trained architect in Columbus. I told him I was designing my dream home. He answered that a layman designing a home is like do-it-yourself brain surgery. He was right, of course. Success is in the details: moldings, placement of electrical outlets, insulation under the roof and in the sidewalls, distance between studs, siding, choice of wood for the deck, storage, etc.

I had no idea how to draw blueprints, so I hired the teenage son of the contractor to do that for me. Fortunately he was competent enough that the contractor could proceed. We worked closely on the thousands of details. What brand of windows to select, what kitchen and bathroom fixtures to install. Where would the septic tank be placed?

The details went on and on, with each decision one of a kind. I had no idea how complex the process would be. Meantime, I was working full time with only weekends to shop and consult.

When we were finished and moved in, I was pleased with the result, though there were a few problems. I forgot to include a front door, and new arrivals had no idea where or how to enter the house—up the side stairs to the living room level or through the basement. I had decided not to have a garage, which was a bad decision. The Ohio winters can be fierce. When blizzards knocked out the electricity, we camped in the living room next to a small Franklin stove and melting snow for toilet flushing.

In the meantime we had befriended a young architect, Whit Tussing, who lived nearby. I commissioned him to correct all my mistakes. He designed a new front to the house, a three-car garage, and a pleasant sitting room. Even with professional help, we had hours and hours of decision making and shopping.

Would I do it again? You bet your bippy.

DAD, AKA THE PSEUDOARCHITECT

By Janice Hudson

Dad is right—he has always been an architect wannabe. For as long as I can remember, Dad always had some building project going.

First effort: The New Room

After the lake was built, he realized there were no large windows to see the lake from the old farmhouse. His answer? He built a Bauhaus-type addition in a very modern style onto the hundred-year-old farmhouse. A new doorway from the old house led to the new space, with steps going to the right and left to enter the room. The most dramatic part of the room was a huge floor-to-ceiling window overlooking the pond. He used canned lighting, of course, with dimmers. He put in a stylish (for the time) free-standing fireplace on one side, which was perfect for winter evenings. As a bonus, under "the new room," as it was called, was a patio. To reach the patio, a spiral staircase descended. Now that was cool.

Second Effort: The Landscape Truck
Arrives at the New House

When Mom and Dad moved back from California in 1974, they moved to the farm and commuted to Columbus to work. They realized the old farmhouse was not suitable for living in the cold winter. Dad had a plan. He had purchased a large painting, Jazz for a Dance, in Palo Alto, but it was too large to fit on any wall in the farmhouse.

This lead to building a new house to display the painting. He picked a hillside that was high enough (he thought) to be able to see the lake from the new house. Unfortunately, it wasn't quite high enough, so he had a local farmer shave off the hill with a bulldozer so the lake was visible. The new house was beautiful, very modern, and spectacular.

After living in Palo Alto, Mom and Dad wanted a hot tub for relaxation and entertaining. So it was to be a built-in, indoor, tiled hot tub adjacent to the bedroom, which could accommodate five or six people. In other words, huge. There was a floor-to-ceiling sliding glass door to see the woods in the back of the house that was opened during soaking, even in the middle of winter. Ah, but there was a problem. How to get enough hot water to fill the thing up? Dad, in his usual way, bought two enormous hot water heaters. In the long run, it was not used often because a slow-running bathtub faucet filled it too slowly. For daily use, there was a normal shower nozzle deep in the hot tub pit.

Mom and Dad parked their cars under the deck that encased the front of the house. In the winter, it proved to be an inadequate shelter. A garage and a new wing with a sitting room soon followed.

At some point, Dad decided he wanted a koi pond, and the landscaping madness began. One of our rituals was my Saturday morning phone call to check in. One morning I was talking to Mom when she said, "Oh, honey, I have to go. The landscape plants just got here." I'm thinking it's a couple of flats and asked why she had to go help. "It's a big truck, honey. Filled with perennials."

That's when I realized our inheritance was flying out the window.

My husband Mark and I began to call the new house "The McCollough Mystery House," named after the Winchester Mystery House in San Jose, California, built by the Winchester daughter who felt that as long as she kept building she would stay alive.

That was followed by the Rock, the McCollough family rock (a huge sandstone boulder that weighed many tons intended to be Dad's tombstone) and a very large sixteen-foot steel sculpture in the pasture overlooking the lake—appropriately lighted, of course.

Third Effort: His Most Mature and Beautiful Work

The Glenford Bank that closed in the stock market crash of 1929 had always fascinated Dad. For years it had been uninhabited, used by the local plumber to store supplies. It was a lovely octagonal brick building with a thirty-five-foot cupola. The tellers' cages were mostly intact, with some of the other original features. The bank vault door had been ripped out and was in the drug store in Thornville.

We had no idea just how far he was to take the bank, which, at the end, was spectacular. Moldings had to be redone by hand. The basement, which ended up being the family room, did not have enough natural light. The answer? Drill through the cement floor under the table in the middle of the rotunda where customers filled out forms. He installed a two-inch-thick glass plate under the table so no one could fall through. A brilliant idea. A million dollars. The upstairs vault was remodeled as a bathroom and required all the plumbing to be drilled through the concrete floor. Of course, since the two-ton vault door was long gone, he searched high and low to find another door. No luck. So he had custom-designed stained glass pocket doors installed.

The ladies' waiting room became the kitchen. The president's office became Mom's office, complete with a huge Arts and Crafts partner's desk where she could work. The gentlemen's waiting room became the dining room, with the original sixty-year-old work table from the bank that he located in the village firehouse, and suitable flatware and china were selected. Gas logs were installed in the fireplace in their bedroom, which I recall was the boardroom. Similar gas logs were installed in the anteroom to the downstairs family room. On the lower level, another bathroom was fashioned from one of eight rooms that fanned out from the octagonal space. A fortune was spent, not only remodeling the building to the true Arts and Crafts style, but included were some authentic Stickley and other Arts and Crafts furniture to furnish this beautiful place.

To stay with the style and times of the bank, he installed period outdoor lamp posts that would have been found on any Midwest main street in the twenties.

But there was a problem. Since the bank was on the village corner, there was no parking. Dad, as usual in his creative mind, bought the house and barn next door. Originally the Smith cottage was to be a guesthouse, but it had deteriorated to the point that it could not be salvaged, so he eyed the dirt-floored barn, which had been meant to become the garage.

This is the part where the phrase "be afraid, be very afraid" comes in. Recall the painting Jazz for a Dance? Obviously his modern paintings wouldn't work in the bank. The dilapidated old barn was transformed into "the loft." Yes, there was a garage, but also a gorgeous two-story ultra-modern New York style loft replacing the rest of the two-story building. And it had a mammoth empty wall. Never say that Dad can't fill in a wall with art. They acquired an enormous triptych by Stanford professor Keith Boyle, which was something like seven feet high and fifteen feet wide. Since they then owned the long side of a whole village block, the expected landscaping was done, and several large sculptures were installed on the lawn.

But there was one last issue. He negotiated with the city fathers for permission to transform the plot across the street and turned it into a park.

In the end, the bank was his most beautiful creation of all. I will always treasure the memory of walking to the bank after sleeping in the loft. Mom and Dad would be sitting in two Stickley chairs drinking their morning coffee with soft classical music playing in the background.

When they moved to Saratoga, I did receive part of my inheritance. I was the recipient of some of my favorite art pieces, as well as some furniture. My home now sports quite a lot of the beautiful contemporary Stickley furniture they acquired while living in the bank. Even though the bank became Dad's "white elephant" (see a previous story), the bank was the most incredible and masterful effort of all his architectural achievements.

ONION PIE—WHO WOULD HAVE THOUGHT IT?

The other night our dining room served onion quiche "made with caramelized onions." I ordered it eagerly, hoping for a taste sensation. The quiche was dismal. The onions were still white, the pie had too much egg custard, and as for taste, it was tasteless and probably frozen. Oh well, you can't go back again, can you?

I had been sent to Germany and Switzerland to find new pediatric pharmaceuticals. My traveling companions were Dr. Mort Soifer, a member of the Ross medical department, and marketing man Mel Karue. Our first stop was in Frankfurt to visit Boeringer Ingelheim. Our second stop was in Zurich. We rented a Volkswagen and started to drive south from Frankfurt. Our route took us through France and a stop in Strasbourg, with its famous cathedral and medieval center. We decided that we could park the car and wander around for a hour before moving on.

The old town was bustling with foot traffic and interesting shops, no doubt to please the tourists. We dropped into a small bistro for a glass of wine. There on the counter was an onion pie. Americans do not consider an onion a vegetable. The onion is a flavor enhancer, an accompaniment to something else. The onion pie was amber, the color of dark honey. We each asked for a slice with a glass of chilled white wine. When we sat down at our table, there were small dishes of caraway seeds and poppy seeds as accompaniments.

My upbringing never included onion pie, nor anything else that might be considered a quiche. The pie was sweet and flavorful, a new experience to enhance my life. The trick of cooking caramelized onions is long, slow cooking. Patience, patience, until they are deeply browned. The white wine was perfect. The treat was heaven sent, but we had to move on to Zurich.

We traveled informally, in jeans and sweaters. Our reservations in Zurich were at the Grand Dolder Hotel, chosen by our secretaries who made the reservations. We arrived about sunset. The hotel sits high above the city in a massive nineteenth-century building that exudes money and haute taste. We pulled up in our Volkswagen and noticed two huge bonfires burning in the front of the hotel, with guards standing at the front door in formal Swiss army dress.

We had arrived the night of the annual Swiss Army officers' ball. As we entered the lobby, hundreds of men in fancy dress clothes and swords and women in long gowns roamed around the first floor waiting for dinner to be served. We felt like unkempt intruders.

We decided that we should go upstairs, shower, shave, and dress in conservative business attire before having dinner. Otherwise, we would have felt disrespectful of the occasion. After dinner we wandered the grand rooms, including the ballroom. It was unreal, like a movie set, with grandly uniformed men and ladies swirling to a Strauss waltz. (It sounded like a Strauss waltz.)

Two treats in one day: onion pie in Strasbourg and an old world fancy ball in Zurich.

Whoever said that business travel was a drag?

PAP FOR AN OLD MAN

Most things in this book are ideas generated in the middle of the night. The writing process usually goes quickly, and then an editing process begins that might take days or weeks to complete. For this topic, this is the third time I have started over. The first draft was too long, detailed, and dull. The second was too short, directionless, and confusing. Both have been trashed, but the topic is worth exploring. It has special meaning for people over eighty.

The topic is "routine," patterns of behavior that might once have been called compulsive behavior but now provide comfort, certainty, and sureness. These behaviors approach ritual but make the day go smoothly. Some call these routines "habits," but they are more than habits for me. They are the cement in the day-to-day. Here are a few examples.

Getting out of bed is not very exciting, but one must follow a proper routine to be sure the first act of the day is a secure one. Turn over, turn off the ceiling fan, reach for your glasses, sit up but wait a few moments so that the blood goes to your head. (Circulation is not what it used to be.) Look out the window to see if it is raining or clear. Then go to the living room to check your blood sugar. If it is too low, immediately eating an Almond Joy may prevent dizziness. If blood sugar is too high, it means that there is no rush to eat breakfast.

Getting dressed and undressed follows closely exact routines. Ordering food in the dining room always ends with the phrase, "and ice tea with lemon." Is that a sin? Taking prescription pills in an orderly fashion prevents making a possibly dangerous error. Routine after routine after routine throughout the day.

Comfort food has been a staple throughout life. Include meatloaf, mashed potatoes, spaghetti with meatballs in tomato sauce, baked potatoes with butter, salt, and pepper, or ice cream in any meal, and life is good. So, too, daily routines provide the same satisfying feeling of comfort for the elderly.

Most importantly, don't mess with our routines. I would be unstable and irritable for hours if you did.

PARIS REDUX

Historian David McCullough has written a book entitled *The Greater Journey* describing the wave of American intellectuals who went to Paris starting in 1830. They went to Paris to work, think, and learn. They did not go for the frivolity and social benefits. They did enjoy the wonderful food, cheap prices, and generally exciting ambiance. It was almost a hundred years before Ernest Hemingway, F. Scott Fitzgerald, Gertrude Stein, and other Americans made Paris their home. They too enjoyed the low expenses, fine wine, and general avant-garde attitudes. By 1900, Paris was dubbed the exciting "City of Lights," with its wide boulevards and the Eiffel Tower.

My life has taken me to Paris six or seven times; so many times I can't recall them all. Sometimes it was vacation, several times for business, and sometimes on visits with relatives and friends. Even though Paris is world renowned, it remains a mystery to me. It has so much history, too many things to visit, so much conventional wisdom and expectations. I remain a stranger.

On one occasion I was the guest of an international association of infant formula manufactures. The meeting was weeklong, but my participation was on a Tuesday and Friday. How to spend my time? I walked and walked and walked as far as I could from my hotel on the rue de Rivoli opposite the Louvre. I roamed the streets and visited stores and shops along the way. In one grocery store, I marveled at a large white ceramic tub filled with ice water and all manner of fresh herbs: basil, dill, thyme, and others. The bakeries nearby featured three-foot-long baguettes, football-sized batards, cookies of all types, and fruit tarts, shiny and delectable. In the next block a store was devoted entirely to white bakeware, where I bought six gratin dishes we used for decades.

On another occasion I decided to visit two famous department stores, Galleries Lafayette and Printemps, to compare the merchandise and prices against the Columbus, Ohio department store, Lazarus. I took the elevator to the top floor and walked through each department until I reached the street level. My conclusion: the offerings were nearly identical to those in Ohio, and the prices were higher. My only purchase was a ceramic bowl of fruit made in Italy.

My wandering took me to the large antique mall near the Palais Royal on the rue de Rivoli opposite an entrance to the Louvre, called Le Louvre des Antiquaires. The 250 stores offered the best of French art, furniture, jewelry, glassware (Lalique), and other high-end treats. On the level above the street, a small food stand served a delicious croque monsieur (grilled ham and cheese), green salad with oil and vinegar, and espresso—the perfect French luncheon.

After several visits to Paris, I regularly went to the Picasso museum to see a Matisse painting that Picasso had exchanged for one of his. It is a decorative piece in warm reds and other bright colors with something like a large crisscross design. All I can think of when I see that Matisse is theft.

Picasso's works are so revealing, from the early academic drawings that are photographic to the later fantasies and jigsaw parts. His ceramics in the lower level are energetic and fun. Look out into the garden, and you see a collection of his stick figure sculptures that are childlike. Picasso could do it all. Give him a bicycle handle and seat, and he would make a bull's head.

Soon after it opened, I visited the Centre Pompidou modern art museum. Like the Guggenheim in New York, the building itself is the work of art: industrial, severe, concrete, glass, and trimmed in brightly colored pipes, stairs, and walkways. Several of the rooms are devoted to Pierre Bonnard, whose paintings I had never studied. I was startled to come across the life-sized nude in the bathtub, soaking in a foot of water, a theme he painted many times. Otherwise, his domestic scenes were a revelation to me, often painted in complex, bright, or muted colors, giving the impression of a happy stay-at-home painter.

The Musée d'Orsay is a huge railway station turned into an art gallery. By the time I went there, I was having some pain walking, and I did not find the renovated building very user-friendly. (Art museums require a lot of walking, especially the Louvre.)

Here's a little advice for those going to Paris for the first time: wander a lot. Eat the bread. It's the best way to understand gay Paree.

ROOT BEER PERMUTATIONS

When I was a child, we always had soft drinks in the ice box: Canada Dry ginger ale, Hires root beer, and Coca-Cola. Mother and Dad used the ginger ale for mixed drinks, and the pop was for the kids.

Hires root beer was my standard of what root beer should be, until Dad's Old Fashioned root beer came along. It was foamy with more body and became our root beer of choice. Soon, roadside A & W root beer restaurants appeared, and after a hot dog and a frosted mug of root beer, we would buy a plastic gallon jug of the soft drink to take home. After a day, the carbonation was lost, and the deflated remnants were thrown away.

When I was young, some people were still making homemade root beer. Once I was invited to go to a friend's cellar to taste some home brew. Conventional wisdom was that if not properly handled, the root beer could blow up, adding a touch of danger to the tasting. We gathered around a case of bottles with white ceramic tops enclosed with a spring wire enclosure. Snapping those back, we tasted the concoction. It was horrible. Yeast was used to promote carbonation, and all I tasted was a malty yeast taste, nothing like our favored Hires.

For a while, something called a "black cow" was a favorite treat. A scoop of vanilla ice cream was put into a large glass, and the glass filled with root beer. The mixture of vanilla ice cream and root beer was delicious. A variant was a root beer milkshake: vanilla ice cream, a touch of milk, and root beer blended to a slushy consistency.

The taste of root beer is complex. Here are the ingredients from an early Hires recipe: birch bark, dog grass, ginger (several types), juniper berries, licorice, sugar, wintergreen, chirreta, hops, sarsaparilla, vanilla, yerba mate, *plus* a secret plant. Today you can buy a root beer extract to make your own, but why would you?

My wife Marian drinks root beer as her favorite pop. The label says it is made by Barg's, a brand I never heard of. I drink Diet Pepsi, but I am pleased that we have chilled root beer available.

Just in case a juvenile urge to make a black cow strikes.

SUCCESSFUL FAILURES

The *Quarterly Journal of Pediatrics* was edited by Irving Wolman, MD. The magazine was rated third behind *Pediatrics* and the *Journal of Pediatrics*. Dr. Wolman and the sales manager of Ross, Dave Cox, would meet from time to time to talk about topics of mutual interest. Not much was known then about mothers' baby-feeding practices once solid foods were introduced into a baby's diet. Dave said that he would be pleased to sponsor a national questionnaire to seek out some authentic data. Dr. Wolman agreed, and Dave called me to tell me I was in charge of the project. My skill was in writing, not in statistics nor in questionnaire development.

I wrote a questionnaire and selected the sample, and we mailed it to hundreds of mothers throughout the United States. Data poured in, and my secretary and I counted responses. After the returns tapered off, I flew to Philadelphia, where Wolman lived, to discuss the findings. He was very pleased, and the data were published. My boss, Dave, was also pleased and decided that we needed to do more studies in maternal behavior, competitive intelligence, and business responses to our promotion.

The trouble was that I was not qualified in market research techniques, so he hired Gil Martinez, who had the necessary skills. He served successfully as director of marketing research for decades. I went back to sales promotion full time.

A few years later, Dave became enamored with a personnel testing device called Activities Vector Analysis (AVA). (Ross used the Wonderlic test to evaluate brain power and AVA to evaluate personality traits.) The AVA was a self-administered test wherein job applicants selected words to describe themselves. These in turn would be used to define basic characteristics such as sociability, aggressiveness, dependency, and basic energy. The author, Walter V. Clarke, required a trained analyst to administer and evaluate the findings.

Guess who that was. Dave selected me for the two-week training course in Florida. Considering this a vacation, I packed up Marian, and we headed to Ft. Lauderdale. I did not expect two weeks of intensive day-and-night meetings in a completely blackened room with the thermostat set at sixtyfive degrees. Clarke was an ogre, but brilliant and opinionated. He berated students for minor infractions and made us feel stupid. One morning Marian knocked at the classroom door to retrieve our car keys. Walter became apoplectic with her and me.

By the end of the two weeks, he was satisfied that I was knowledgeable enough, and I was certified as an AVA analyst.

When I returned to Columbus, I was the person designated to analyze all tests. I wrote dozens and dozens of reports used in hiring all new personnel nationwide. The company was growing, and eventually a human resources department was founded. Once again I returned to sales promotion and advertising full time.

Why I was selected as the company guinea pig, I'll never know. When sensitivity training became a popular fad, I was the first person to be sent to the course at Oberlin, Ohio. Dave thought I was much too insensitive (neurotic?); it turned out that I was overly sensitive and could sense emotions before the trainers could. Oh well. I returned to sales promotion and advertising full time.

Every once in a while, Dave would have an insight. He decided that we should enter the medical food business, and he called me in to see if I could do anything with his idea. This time it was low-salt, low-fat cheddar cheese. After a little exploration, I found a processed cheese company in Wapakoneta, Ohio, home of Neil Armstrong, who had walked on the moon. The Fisher Cheese Company was delighted to cooperate with this new venture. I wrote the promotional materials, selected the mailing lists of doctors, and started a small mail-order business. The experiment was a complete flop. We never sold enough cheese to cover costs, and I was once again able to go back to sales promotion and advertising full time.

I was not always successful in sales promotion, either. One sales cycle, I invented a sales aid I called a "cube-octahedron." Imagine a colorful six-inch-square box with every corner clipped off. The flat sides were used to describe basic ingredients: lactose, protein, and vegetable oils. The clipped corners featured other product preference features. The theme was "integrated nutrition." The only trouble was that the salesmen were too embarrassed to show it to pediatricians. One of my peers, Jim McCall, was so amused that he had one imbedded in an eight-inch Plexiglas plastic cube to remind me that my good ideas were not always wonderful.

Something went right. The business grew from twelve million to a billion annual dollars. My peers and managers kept me in check … usually.

THE BETSY COMMITTEE

The most important event in my business career occurred in the early sixties. I worked for a small company in Columbus by the name of the Moores and Ross Dietetic Laboratories. They manufactured an infant formula, Similac, and an infant cereal, Cerevim. After a brief stint in the field as a salesman, I was brought into the home office after my army service to write and prepare sales materials. In 1951, the company sales were $12 million dollars. Ten years later they were $30 million. The company was managed entirely by the Ross family, and their fortunes were dependent on the success of the company.

Mel Ross was president, and his brother, Dick, was general manager. Mel was the "money man," and Dick was the "people person." Mel saw two problems. The company was growing fast, and it needed large infusions of cash to fund growth. He also realized that the Ross family wealth was not diversified, so he asked Dick to seek merger possibilities.

Our products were sold to doctors, but the business had originally grown through the milk and ice cream business. Dick started making contacts with both food and pharmaceutical companies. Contacts were made with

Smuckers and Beechnut. On the pharmaceutical side, he contacted Pfizer. Our return on investment was very high, so the brothers felt they might receive some good offers. Pfizer was very interested and made the first bid. Mel liked the offer very much, but Dick was hesitant. Mr. Keen, head of Pfizer, intended to dissolve the Ohio business and move the staff to New York. Dick did not want to move to New York, and the bid was put on hold.

Because I was creating sales material, I was occasionally brought along to describe that part of the business. The day we were to make a presentation to Beechnut, our sales manager, Dave Cox, had a back spasm, and we left him at the company New York apartment on the floor with a pot to pee in and the door cracked so a messenger could deliver some Miltown, one of the first muscle relaxants and tranquilizers. Dick Ross and I made a presentation, but we felt that the Beechnut management was not representing their financial status honestly. We backed away.

A few months later, Abbott Laboratories, headquartered in North Chicago, showed interest. Ross formed the "Betsy Committee" as our merger team. Betsy Ross contained the name Ross, so Betsy became the code name for the activity. Those included were Dave Cox (representing sales and management), Gil Martinez (marketing research), Dr. Jack Filer (medical), Tom McCollough (sales promotion and advertising), and perhaps one other.

The Abbott team was headed by Ted Ledder, President of Abbott Pharmaceuticals, and a handful of others whose names I cannot remember. From the beginning the merger looked like a fit. Our ad agency in New York, William Douglas McAdams, serviced drug companies only, and our approach was scientific. Our sales were then $32 million, and Abbott's were $136 million, four times our sales. Abbott had an excellent reputation, and Mr. Cain, their CEO, was best described as "classy and upscale."

One day Mr. Cain played golf with another pharmaceutical CEO on the North Shore of Chicago. (Schering?) He suggested that the two of them merge their companies. The Ross negotiations came to a screeching halt, much to our disappointment. In time, though, the two men argued about who would be the CEO of a merged company, and that merger fell apart. A few months later, Abbott reopened our talks. Our merger was consummated in 1964.

In one of our meetings, I made an "I have a dream speech." I said we could envision Ross as the pediatric arm of Abbott, because we had great rapport with pediatricians. Little did we know that Abbott would never give us their best drugs with pediatric doses. Instead, they foisted their languishing vitamin brand on us, Vi-Daylin, and a very old penicillin product we renamed Pediacillin.

Ross prospered significantly, and we were the Abbott cash cow. For at least a decade, we provided 51 percent of Abbott's profit. This was critical, because Abbott intravenous solutions ran into a cracked glass problem and had serious, serious financial problems. We were raking in cash so fast that Mr. Cain once said to Dick Ross,

"I know you are making more money than you have reported." I knew. I had just prepaid a four-million-dollar advance purchase of printing for the following year. Ross did have some leverage, because Dick Ross was the largest stockholder of the merged companies and a member of the Abbott board of directors. Generally, we were left to run the business without interference.

However, we always felt we were treated as the country cousins. We had a Twin Beechcraft airplane, but they insisted the plane be kept in North Chicago rather than Columbus. When money got tight, they insisted on Ross price increases to bring in more cash.

When I retired, our division sales were at about a billion dollars.

Not bad for the hicks in the hinterland.

THE ESSENCE OF
SAN FRANCISCO

Is it the Golden Gate, Coit Tower, Fishersman's Wharf, Union Square, Lombard Street, and Alcatraz that typifies San Francisco? No, it is *Beach Blanket Babylon*, the satiric musical revue that has been running since 1974.

When we have visitors from out of town, we buy tickets to the show for a Saturday matinee. The performance is held in the Club Fugazi, a theater configured as a night club. Small tables are set in front of the stage, and before the curtain, the ushers take a drink order. The seats on the first floor are not reserved, so an hour before the doors open, a line begins to form in front of the theater. When we were still mobile, we would wait in the line, hoping to get a good seat. Later, as our legs weakened, we bought reserved seats in the balcony, so we could enter the theater when the crush was over. The show was so popular that a rich merchant, I. Magnum, had a box made at the front of the balcony. In our waning years, that is where we usually sat.

Before the show, we dine at the Italian restaurant on the corner of the same block. We always overeat. The first course is a minestrone soup, followed by a tossed salad, after which comes an entrée of some classic Italian meat or fish course. We pass on dessert because we have been wolfing down crispy Italian bread with butter all through dinner.

Then to the theater. Because they have two shows on Saturday, the theater darkens exactly on time. A side door opens, and three trumpet players in Blues Brothers dark glasses, blaring a march, enter with the pit band. A great keyboardist, a drummer, and a few others blast out some snappy tunes. The show begins. The plot is flimsy. Snow White is looking for a husband anywhere and everywhere, in France, in Italy, in the Carribean, in Africa. None of that matters. The show is a montage of spoofs on contemporary popular culture and the people who are designated as famous: Hillary Clinton, Oprah, Prince Charles and Camilla, Tiger Woods, and a gang of entertainers like Michael Jackson, Barbra Streisand, and Lady Gaga. Each is portrayed with an exaggerated hairdo and some sort of joke or pun that reflects their personality. Between the blackouts, musical numbers include old standards belted out and danced by some fine singers. The finale is always the same. Some ladies appear in outlandish hats eight feet wide and six feet tall. The hats are animated, and even a small train runs around a Christmas tree during the holidays.

The last song is "San Francisco," sung by the whole cast, which bridges to a double time version that exudes energy and good feeling. The applause is long and heartfelt. The lobby fills with happy, smiling people pouring out into the street.

In recent weeks I have noticed that they are advertising the show on television. Does that mean that the house is not packed as usual? I can't imagine San Francisco without *Beach Blanket Babylon*.

PS: Snow White eventually marries Elvis Presley. What a pair! PPS: During the show, a Jewish mother tells Snow White to marry a "rich doctor." Who shows up? An African "witch doctor."

If you aren't amused by puns, you better not go.

THE NIGHT I TRIED TO TURN OFF THE MOON

Is it true that dreams are our mind's method for ridding us of worries? Or are they a method to keep us asleep? Or, as Freud believed, are dreams a pathway to understand our psyche, with or without an analyst? Whatever. Almost all people dream some of the time, adding a surreal dimension to our lives.

By and large my dreams reveal a certain amount of stress. Exact repetition of the same dream is unusual, but three themes reappear. Dreams of life on our farm; dreams of my former work life; and dreams about Glenford, the small village where we owned a weekend home.

The farm was a hill farm with a one-hundred-year old frame farmhouse. The recurring dream usually involves traveling there to discover that development had created new roads, there was excessive bulldozing to accommodate the quarry nearby, and some rundown, unoccupied old houses had appeared next to our farm house. Our privacy is compromised, to my dismay.

The most recent dream about the village of Glenford involved a group of men, mostly members of the Lions Club. Every year we sponsored an old-fashioned steam show to raise funds. (We rented a dozen steam tractors and participants brought their favorite large and small steam engines for display.) The show was usually held in back of the schoolyard on Lions property. In my dream, this festival was held in a remote, secluded grove of trees. The trees were dying off, and no one could explain why. Glen Hursey, former principal of the school, said that the trees had been properly trimmed and cared for, so the problem was a mystery and unsolved.

The thematic dreams about work are typically about travel to places all over the world. On arrival at the airport for the return trip, I can't find the tickets to board the plane. Anxious discussions ensue, and I wake. (Frequently I am accompanied by a work-related buddy, such as Dewey Sehring or Howard Scholick.) These three thematic dreams are infrequent, but are very real when they occur. And yes, they are in color.

Dreams remind me of the experience that occurs when my blood sugar gets too low, usually caused by taking too much insulin. Things begin to go fuzzy, and self-awareness flees. Marian asks, "Why didn't you call me to help you?" The answer is that you do not think clearly when you are hypoglycemic, and rational thought disappears. Everything is just a muddle.

I recently had an interesting dream-like experience. It was not a dream nor a hypoglycemic attack. It was a type of out-of-body experience.

The moon was full, and the bedroom was brightly lit. I turned over, and the bright moon was shining directly into my eyes. I reached for the ceiling fan remote and tried to turn the moon off with the stop button. But I turned on the ceiling light and had to wake up enough to turn the light off.

The moon was still glowing, and I laughed at the absurdity of my action. Oh well, at eighty-three we do some silly things.

THINGS I HAVE NEVER DONE

I have never parachuted from an airplane.

I note this because the elder George Bush did that on his eightieth birthday. I am eighty-three, and the dare never occurred to me. Am I cowardly? Yes.

I have never eaten an octopus.

Once on a business trip to Lebanon, I was taken out for a three-hour lunch of delicacies favored by our sales force there. The octopi in an oily marinade were only several inches wide. Am I cowardly? Yes.

I have never owned a boat.

Not perfectly true. On Marian's birthday, the Behns bought her a metal rowboat for our farm pond, the *Maid Marian*. In some states the spouse owns half of the estate, so technically I owned half an aluminum rowboat. But I was never tempted to make that expensive leap to sail boat, motorboat, or other boat.

I have never learned to speak a foreign language fluently.

> Oh, how I wanted to. I studied high school Spanish, college Spanish, and hired a private Spanish tutor for a year. Sure, I could say, "Como esta usted." But when native speakers spoke rapidly in return, my head became a blur. I blame it on my fuzzy hearing, but some people like me just don't have an ear for a second language.

I have never been to Australia or New Zealand.

> While it true that I circumnavigated the earth by going to a pediatric convention in New Delhi, I never had occasion to go Down Under. Neither on a vacation nor on business did I get to see the opera house in Sydney, the great Barrier Reef, or Ayers Rock. But I've seen them all in the National Geographic magazine. Cross Australia off the list.

I have never scuba dived.

> Basically I have always had a fear of water, or more precisely, of being thrown into water before I could swim. Then too, swimming water always seems too cold to me. We've been to enough places that had scuba diving available, but nothing attracted me to it.

I have never owned a ruby.

> Garnets yes, rubies no. Once when visiting the Dominican Republic, I bought Marian a pear-shaped

piece of amber as large as a real pear. We had it set in a silver setting that mimicked a clinging vine. The stone had many insect inclusions, and Marian wore it when we went to formal events. We had a jewelry heist, and it was stolen. I bought another large piece of amber to replace the loss, but Marian never liked to wear the substitute.

I have never worked on an archeological dig.

We have visited many digs but never worked in one. Our trips to Turkey and Israel let us visit active digs— dirty, hot, boring. The magazine *Biblical Archeology* presents an annual summary of open digs-for-hire that anyone with the airfare and a budget can go to for a month or so when the professors are there. The dig photos usually show young people sifting dirt or brushing away dust with a small brush. It sounds glamorous, but I'm guessing it is not.

I have never cheated on my wife.

And I suspect that she has never cheated on me. I've had opportunities. Many of my hosts in foreign countries (Lebanon and the Philippines, for example) would ask if I would like to arrange for a hooker for the night. I guess they thought that all red-blooded American men would appreciate the service. All I could think of was the possible complications. It was no big deal.

I have never owned a Rolls-Royce.

> We always lived well, but never lavishly. I bought cars that were utilitarian and reliable. Clothes were chosen because they were suitable, but never fanciful. My preference was to live in a nice house that had its own points of interest. Marian worked most of our married life, providing the extra income to enable us to have many small luxuries and vacations.

I have never worn contact lenses.

> My daughter Elizabeth could not wait until she was twelve and her eyes had matured. Then she could have contact lenses and get rid of her thick glasses, which she was certain scared off beaus. I thought she looked cute in glasses, but she insisted that only contacts would make her attractive to the boys. Millions of people wear contact lenses, but the thought of putting that plastic disk on your eyeball daily was repulsive to me. At about age thirty-five, I noticed that the telephone pages were blurred. I went to Woolworth's and bought reading spectacles. I started with the weakest magnification and ended years later with the most powerful glasses you could buy for twelve dollars.

The moral of this story is that you can only cram so many events and things into a lifetime. There are a lot of "nevers," but these are balanced with the many "dids" and "hads" over a lifetime.

"I'D WALK A MILE FOR A CAMEL"

old cigarette advertising slogan

Mother and Dad were chain smokers. Mother smoked Sir Walter Raleighs because they had a coupon on the back that could be redeemed for prizes, especially glassware that filled our cupboard. Dad had a strange cigarette habit. He would roll out both ends of a cigarette, depositing the unused leaves in flower pots. When he lit up, a hot flame would produce a spectacular fire and presumably a hot taste.

It never occurred to me to smoke until I went to college, where I was surrounded by returning veterans of World War II, most of whom had taken up the habit because the government provided a few smokes with every K-ration in the field. In response, I believed that all teen-aged boys should learn to smoke cigarettes. I bought a pack of Lucky Strikes and spent one afternoon walking up and down Broad Street in Philadelphia practicing puffing on one after another. Mother stopped smoking cold turkey when Dad became ill, so I knew that I couldn't smoke at home. I hated the taste and couldn't imagine why anyone would want to light up. Now of college age, pipe smoking was another attractive alternative.

I bought a cheap pipe and some flavored tobacco. It was like smoking perfume, but the tobacco taste was masked. After practicing for a month, I took the pipe home and lit up in the living room. Mother smelled the smoke and ran into the room saying, "What do you think you are doing? Put that out, and never smoke here again." After a few months of trying to keep the damned pipe lit, I quit anyway. My hope of looking scholarly was dashed.

After college, I never smoked again—until 1961, when we bought the old hill farm. We purchased our supplies at Luke Swinehart's store in the middle of Glenford, a small village with a general store, several churches, and a schoolhouse. Luke offered a supply of cigars for the mostly rural population. One day I bought a pack of Swisher Sweets, a small flavored cigar, at four for ten cents. I got hooked and started smoking them on weekends.

At work, most executives smoked, but I was embarrassed smoking cheap cigars, so I went to the tobacco store on Long Street and bought some twenty-five-cent cigars to smoke at the office, particularly at meetings. Slowly, my tastes escalated, and before long I was smoking one-dollar Nicaraguan cigars and buying them by the box. Now every cigar smoker in the building would come by to "borrow" a cigar. And my usage was no longer contained to the office. I was smoking cigars at home, on weekends, and in the car—close to twelve cigars a day. Because I didn't inhale, I reasoned that I was doing no harm. But other issues arose. My good clothes were full of little burn holes, and I was getting hoarse, particularly in the morning. By calculating the cost of my cigars, I was spending $2,000 a year for a habit I didn't like.

So I stopped cold turkey. Buying paintings was a more satisfying way to spend money than smoking. It was an easy decision. A good thing, too. The company went smoke free, and I was a step ahead of my smoker friends.

Surgeon General Koop announced the medical dangers of smoking to the nation, and the culture of smoke-free society took hold. Now like all reformed smokers, I hate the smell of cigarette, cigar, or pipe smoke. (It has not yet occurred to young people that smoking pot is also "smoking.") This too will pass.

New problems arose. It's a given that when people stop smoking, they will gain weight. I did. Could it be that smoking secession has caused our national obesity crisis? Think about it. (Perhaps I should write an essay about the dangers of unintended consequences.)

Cigars are international, and when I traveled, I would smoke the local favorites. For example, when in Italy I tried a cigar called Toscano Antica. The crude cigar has been fabricated for two centuries. It is hard as a rock, enormously pungent with bold flavor, and aged for a year. You buy them by the fistful, and the tobacconist wraps them in paper. They are lethal and not recommended.

Cuban cigars were illegal and would be confiscated if brought through US customs. One year we were in Geneva shopping for the holidays. Marian went to the world-famous tobacco store, Davids, to buy twelve Cuban cigars for me. The clerk asked her whether she wanted the bands removed, meaning that if they were coming back to the States, they could not be identified. No problem. Some friends and I smoked all twelve during the New Year's Eve weekend. They were nothing special, in spite of their outrageous cost, but it did give us a tingle to smoke an illegal treat.

A Camel slogan proclaimed, "More doctors smoke Camels than any other cigarette." I wonder whether the American Medical Association received a royalty for that questionable endorsement.

WHAT WE LIVE FOR

Kurt Vonnegut, as he aged, offered two thoughts for the well-being of mature persons. First, he suggested that the nuclear family is not large enough to provide the support and comfort we all need. Consider the complicated relationships between husbands and wives, and between parents and their children. More is needed, he proposed.

Subsequently, he invented a word that has become part of modern man's vocabulary: the karass, the people that we randomly become linked with throughout life, such as work groups, church groups, hobby groups, and service groups. He believed there is a mystical and unexplainable bond involved, a bond that gives us sustenance, definition, pleasure, and comfort.

For example, consider our SRC writers' group. All of us have unique narratives as well as different interests, backgrounds, and personalities. Yet the bonding among us is palpable, as we look forward to each month's meetings and the varied and diverse offerings presented, slowly revealing our inner lives to one another. Multiply these feelings by everyone you relate to—the bridge club, the committees you serve on, frequent table mates, golf partners, neighbors, relatives, and friends. We weave a sustaining web around us that gives meaning to our lives. "Family" is great, but not enough. We need the karass.

We also live for the anticipation of many pleasures. For example, the cycle of the seasons provides sustaining joys. The crepe myrtle is blooming. (Could anything be more beautiful?) The peaches are ripe, sweet, and delicious. The sweet corn is in, reminding us of childhood dinners with stacks of corn on the cob slathered in melted butter with salt and pepper. Remember?

Books and reading take on new meaning. Old books, new books, classics, books of no consequence, and books that are life-changing. They all are valuable. The more you read, the more discriminating your evaluation of writing becomes. A book that engages you and draws you into its fabric is a revelation. You feel that you have not wasted your time and that your life has been enhanced.

We seek laughter and humor. Friends send silly or risqué jokes via e-mail, and we pass them on to those you think might enjoy them, all the while building a circle of laughter among a unique karass. In the evenings we watch Jon Stewart and Steven Colbert. Why? Because they convey a feeling of being an insider. Their frequent use of ribald humor pleases that sense of being a sixth-grader hearing an off-color joke for the first time.

For the same reason, I enjoy a cable reality show entitled *Pawn Stars* on the History Channel. Most of the program is unscripted and features three members of a slightly dysfunctional family in Las Vegas who run a pawn shop. They have an employee, Chumley, who could be written into a sitcom. He is dumb and silly but wise, in an overweight, slovenly, tattooed body. The show has the highest rating on the cable networks, and I live for Monday night when the newest shows are presented. Reruns sustain me the rest of the week.

Thirty years ago it would be implausible that I would become a computer aficionado, but I have. The computer permits me to have an electronic karass. I read newspapers, shop on Amazon, send for supplies, and search old and new blogs for information and opinions of all stripes. When my mind wants a rest, I play solitaire and mah jong while I reorganize my disorderly mind. Those mindless games are similar to yoga and tai chi; they permit me to center when I am disrupted. Our computer address book names friends and relatives that constitute another living web.

There is something special that I live for at assisted living. We now reside among a group of people who either have some physical or mental deficiency. If you listen and watch carefully, you can reconstruct their lives as they once were, whole and active. They too become part of the personal circle surrounding you. Dementia can be amusing. Did you hear the joke of the aged lady who was stopped for speeding? "Where are you going in such a hurry?" the cop asked. "Well sir, I have to speed before I forget where I am going."

Whether we realize it or not, our life is not a twenty-five-piece jigsaw puzzle. It is a thousand-piece jigsaw puzzle. We are surrounded by a huge and mystical karass.

Enjoy.

IN SUM

Would I like to be a teenager again? Hell no!

Would I like to live my life over again? Hell no!

At eighty-three I find myself assessing how my life went, where the highlights and problems occurred. On balance, life has brought more ups than downs, but I have no desire to relive any of it. I did not expect to live this long. By chance, my mother's longevity genes have prevailed. (She died at ninety. Her triplet father lived to eighty-four.)

I was born on May 5, 1929, the fifth day of the fifth month. I thought that five was my lucky number. It wasn't. I lost every bet based on the number five.

My mother and father had hard times during the 1930s depression, but I never had any sense that we would miss meals or not have clothes nor a place to live. Mother sewed outfits, and Dad had to commute to New York from Philadelphia to find work. But I never sensed any tension about it.

Mother's father lost his wealth in a real estate collapse during the Great Depression. After my maternal grandmother died, he lived with his surviving children for six months at a time. He shared my bed when he was with us. Mother gave him fifty cents a day. He smoked one White Owl cigar daily and walked to a local bar to have one shot of whiskey. In other words, we lived as most people lived in the Depression—at the edge, but not sullenly.

I liked going to elementary school and did okay through junior high school, at which time Dad died of a massive stroke. Schooling started filling in the void, and I latched on to several teachers as father figures. And I became involved in school activities, like pep rallies, school newspapers, etc.

But I always felt a little shy and inferior, probably because of my twin brothers, five years older, who were athletically inclined. They were macho, and when we played catch, they threw the ball too hard for me to be comfortable. I was, in the eyes of my parents, the baby to be protected.

Somewhere along the way, I concluded that the twins could own the realm of sports. I would get smart. However, my grades were never very high, and I never competed with the very bright kids. High school had highs and lows. Study was never my strong suit. I rarely did homework at home, preferring to study during the lunch hour and squeak through. But I was in everything, writing a gossip column for the school newspaper, acting in the senior play, head football manager, etc. When the senior class voted, I was elected as the most outstanding student in the senior class.

At that time I was very sexually naïve. In those days, no one talked about pregnancy, and I was very shy and never asked any questions. I learned about sex from a blind teenager, Tom Good, who lived down the street. (I was a reader for him). He went to the local blind school and was sleeping with a young blind girl. He was very graphic about how it all worked, and my friends and I were fascinated. Sex talk was taboo at home. Dad never said a word to me. You would expect that my older brothers would have spilled the beans. (When I was ten, they were fifteen.) Nothing.

Much later I met a nice young girl at the young adult group at church. In time we married. Knowing more about sex, we had two unique and interesting daughters. I was a fortunate man. Marian is completely guileless, a willing partner to my machinations, and a great mother to the children. We nicknamed her "Mother Earth." What more could a man ask?

It was assumed that I would go to college and then to medical school. I took a number of pre-med courses but found that I had a hard time getting through the quantitative chemistry and physics courses. The veterans were coming home from World War II, and the competition was keen. Besides, I knew that we didn't have much money, and I didn't want to be a burden.

After graduation from the University of Pennsylvania with a major in zoology, I applied to several pharmaceutical companies, Burroughs-Wellcome, Vicks, and a small company in Columbus, Ohio, then called M & R Dietetic

Laboratories. I had several offers, but I selected the M & R Labs because they paid $275 a month plus a car. In all I worked there forty-three years.

A word about chance in life. Can any of us ever make sense of personal decision making? Could I know that I was joining a small, underdeveloped company with few products, a bit of hope and a lot of debt, or that the business would grow exponentially to become a billion-dollar division of Abbott Laboratories, and that I would become a millionaire based on the stock options I was granted? None of this was planned.

One day the president of the company told me that someday I would be president of Abbott. However, I learned through the years that I was far too insecure and sensitive to match the insensitivity and big ego required of the presidential job. I was an exceptional staff person. I had the capacity to take the vision of a leader and find a way to implement and make it work, and it worked. I never asked for a raise, or a staff, or a promotion. They just kept coming.

After joining M & R, I was drafted in 1951 into the army during the Korean war. I liked the army and did well enough to win a commission, and spent a year and a half in Germany running a small health clinic in Butzbach, north of Frankfurt. During that time I wrote to the sales manager of the company frequently. After discharge, he asked me to come to Columbus to prepare sales materials. Eventually I became the company's first Vice President of Advertising and Sales Promotion.

A psychiatrist friend, Hugh Missildine, described to me a characteristic that I exhibited he called "ascendant behavior." I joined the church choir and was elected president. I was a deacon, then an elder, then the clerk of session. I became involved in the civil rights movement and was selected as the Chairman of the Columbus Urban Education Coalition.

Back at M & R (now the Ross Division of Abbott Laboratories), we never seemed to have trouble achieving a sales gain of 10 percent a year, and often a lot more. We became the cash cow of the Abbott Corporation and generally were left alone. But we always had tension and problems of one sort or another to cause sleepless nights. We were led by a brilliant but very neurotic man, Dave Cox, who managed by keeping us off-center and upset.

About 1970 I quit Ross and joined the National Program for Educational Leadership, a federal program whose purpose it was to bring non-traditional leaders into the educational reform movement. After eighteen months studying school systems, I was offered a job to head up a redesign program in the Palo Alto School System in California. It was a mistake of NPEL to let me take that job. The school system was already performing in the high ninetieth percentile by all measures. The system really didn't need reinventing. I applied for and received a federal grant to cover all expenses for the project, so we spent three years in massive participatory planning activities receiving and organizing opinions from students, parents, teachers, and administrators.

(Here is an important secret: When you put thirty kids in a classroom with one adult, there are constraints that can't be altered. The teacher is part cop, part instructor, part substitute parent. Schools can't change as long as that classroom pattern prevails.)

Living in Palo Alto was a treat, thanks to the weather, culture, adventure, more study, and learning. But as the redesign project terminated, Dave Cox called and asked me to return to the company to handle a new kind of problem he was having caused by selling infant formula in developing countries. Again with little forethought, I said sure. For the next five years, I traveled the globe, interacted with social critics, and managed the conflicting dynamics among several divisions of Abbott. We were successful. The business never suffered, and eventually the problem evaporated.

Now what to do with Tom? Okay, let's make him the house ethicist with the title of Director of Business Practices. I vetted advertising, mentored young executives, headed up a number of organizational development projects (OD), managed the crisis management team, and became one of the persons to go to when unexpected problems arose. When asked what I did for a living, I couldn't give a cohesive answer—nothing and everything. And now retirement.

The first years of retirement brought serious health problems. We had enough money not to worry about the future, but how and where we would spend that future was unclear. Marian and I decided that we didn't want to burden our kids with elderly parents. We started looking at retirement communities. Janice was the more settled daughter living in the Bay Area, and we loved California. We eventually settled at the Saratoga Retirement Community in Saratoga, California, first in independent living for four years and then in assisted living.

It has been a long and satisfying life. It would be wonderful to eliminate all the problems and worries we had along the way (e.g., Marian's breast cancer), but that is not possible.

An important part of a lifetime are the few close friends who have enriched our lives. The emphasis is on the word "few"—those few who have shared a hot tub, naked; those who have traveled or vacationed with us; those with whom we have shared rites and other extraordinary events. Names are not as important as those wonderful shared experiences.

"The moving finger writes and moves on."

Would I like to live it all over again? Hell no!

I'm tired.

AFTERWORD

Sunsets are a metaphor for the end of things, but they may be occasions for a special event or a memory. Watching a sunset in Sanibel, Hawaii, or Sea Ranch brings a quiet moment and a bit of thrill when the sun disappears below the horizon. At that moment one hopes to see the "green flash," a brief flash of electric green light like a sudden insight, probably a negative afterimage.

The decision to write this three-volume memoir was one of those flashes. At this age energy falters, and one wonders what new thing can be accomplished. The writing has provided the experience of examining the arc of my life, the little and big things, the successes and failures, the happy and sad times,

I was fortunate to live in a golden age after World War II when the economy grew steadily, when America was at peace (except Korea and Vietnam), and when important social change provided me the opportunity to participate in a number of experiments. I am grateful too for the remarkable success of the company I worked for, providing fascinating work with an unusual boss and a gaggle of interesting peers and a secure retirement.

With the advent of the Internet, I am able to remain in touch with many of the associates and friends who have made my life interesting. Who could have guessed that a command "send" could instantly put you in touch with England or Israel?

After the sun sets, an orange glow fills the sky.

That's us.